THE INMAN FAMILY

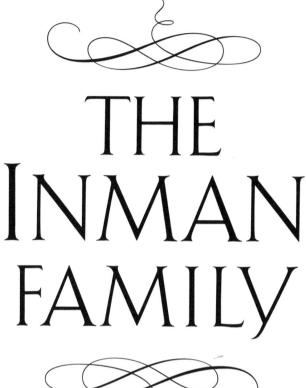

THE
INMAN
FAMILY

An Atlanta Family
from Reconstruction
to World War I

Tammy Harden Galloway

MERCER UNIVERSITY PRESS | 2002
MACON, GEORGIA

ISBN 0-86554-755-6
MUP/H567

First edition

Book design by Mary-Frances Burt, Burt & Burt Studio

The paper in this publication meets the minimum requirements
of American National Standard for Information Sciences—
Permanence of Paper for Printed Materials, ANSI Z39.48-1984.

Library of Congress Cataloging-in-Publication Data

Galloway, Tammy.
  The Inman family : an Atlanta family from Reconstruction to
World War I / Tammy Harden Galloway.
    p. cm.
Includes bibliographical references (p.) and index.
  ISBN 0-86554-755-6 (hardcover : alk. paper)
1. Inman family. 2. Atlanta (Ga.)—Biography. 3. Atlanta
(Ga.)—Social life and customs. 4. City and town life—
Georgia—Atlanta—History. 5. Businessmen—Georgia—
Atlanta —Biography. 6. Politicians—Georgia—Atlanta—
Biography. 7. Elite (Social sciences)—Georgia—Atlanta—
Biography. 8. Atlanta (Ga.)—Economic conditions. 9. United
States —History—Civil War, 1861-1865—Influence. I. Title
  F294.A853 A24 2002
  975.8'23104'0922—dc21

2002001380

TABLE OF CONTENTS

INTRODUCTION

An examination of the effect the Civil War had on Atlanta and the state of Georgia helps explain the conditions in the city after the war that enabled energizing businessmen to prosper. Before the Civil War, Atlanta, like other Southern towns, was largely tied to the agricultural economy and dependent on Northern industries to buy Southern raw materials and to produce finished products that Southern merchants sold in their dry goods stores. Until the eve of the war, the South continued this practice of producing raw materials to be used in Northern factories. A few years before the war started, investors and merchants began to consider the possibility of establishing factories in Atlanta to reduce the city's dependence on the North for manufactured goods, but the war began before the idea could take a full grip on the city. Ironically, the war had its own way of helping further the idea. With the war underway and the blockades in place, raw materials remained in the South while finished products were hard to find and expensive when available. Merchants attempted to meet the demands of their consumers by blockade running or by founding manufacturing businesses in which they had little or no experience.

Not long after setting out to make Atlanta a city of industrial importance to the Confederacy, the manufacturers soon realized that the South did not possess all the necessary raw materials to produce the quantity and quality of the products formerly made in the North to which their clients were accustomed. By restricting the use of iron for any purpose other than weapons, the Confederate government hurt these young companies. Also holding back production was the shortage of skilled labor in the Atlanta area. Southern skilled workers, limited in number, were off at war, and available workers to operate the new factories were few. Perhaps if the manufacturers had been able to employ the skilled craftsmen and machinists needed, their production rate might have been much higher.[1]

Reflecting this busy manufacturing setting was the rapid expansion of the population of Atlanta. In 1860 the population more than doubled, increasing from 10,000 to 22,000, and it was with this new growth that Atlanta officially became a city.[2] Along with this growth spurt, Atlanta became unruly due to its growing pains.

The increase in the population and the rise in crime did not lead to the expansion of the local police department. As the war progressed, the Confederate armies called on all able-bodied men between the ages of 15 and 50 to serve, leaving the city and the safety of its inhabitants in the hands of older men and inexperienced youths. Gambling, prostituting, suspected spying, and indecent exposure were the most common grounds for arrest. More serious crimes also increased during this period, including homicide, assault, and larceny.[3]

The physical destruction of Atlanta caused by the war had a profound impact on the mobility of new men after the war. Shells were fired at least once every five minutes on the night of 11 August and hit many private homes and businesses as well as military targets, according to one of Sherman's aides.[4] By the middle of August, with the exception of the buildings in the southern and southeastern part of the city, shells had struck almost all the structures; however, Northern forces were not responsible for all the destruction. Under orders of the Confederate leaders, soldiers destroyed railroad equipment and all the ammunition and military supplies stored in Atlanta, and they sent the gun-producing machinery South.[5] Confederate cavalrymen leveled the Atlanta Rolling Mill, one of the early signs of industry in Atlanta. They were also in charge of destroying seven locomotives and 150 railroad cars filled with ammunition. From 40 miles away the explosion was heard, and the Union army claimed that this explosion and fire was what destroyed many of the houses and businesses in Atlanta.[6] Sherman repeatedly denied having destroyed anything that was not of military importance to the Confederacy, but officially he had ordered all the main buildings in Atlanta burned.[7] By the night of 15 November, one of Sherman's officers wrote, the buildings that had covered over two hundred acres were in ruins or in flames. To the eyes of this soldier, Atlanta existed no more.[8] Sherman's army evacuated Atlanta on 16 November and began the March to the Sea. Sherman commented on the state of Atlanta as the march began: "Behind us lay Atlanta, moldering and in ruins, the black smoke rising high in air, and hanging like a pall over the ruined city."[9]

Following the war, scenes of destruction and desolation marked much of Atlanta. The forest that had once surrounded Atlanta was thin. Homes and businesses lay in ashes, and fields remained uncultivated and full of weeds. What little livestock that survived was weak and thin, and Sherman's ties lined what used to be the railroads, which were the life-lines of the city. Union soldiers would pull up the rails of tracks, heat them over bonfires, and twist them around nearby trees. Sherman felt that it was very important to destroy the railroads, and he "gave it [his] own personal attention."[10] They served as just one of the many reminders of the recent visitors. For Atlanta and the surrounding area, it was time to rebuild.

With the excellent rail connections that had once run through Atlanta, there was no question about where to start. Rebuilt with a common gauge, the railroads increased the South's ability to move its raw materials, and by rail those crops went to Atlanta. The common location of raw materials and transportation was also the most logical place to build new factories. The city naturally became a distribution center for a variety of agricultural products, among them cotton. Railroads, now pushing into the interior where cotton began to appear on newly culti-vated land, had been the desire of many cotton traders before the war and were now becoming a reality. Trade grew between the rural areas of the South and Atlanta, and soon there was a need for other types of businesses including financial institutions such as Atlanta's first national bank, founded in 1865, and the Georgia National Bank, founded in 1866.[11] The founding of these and many other businesses were to meet the "financial needs of a growing new economy."[12] The state also felt the need for financial institutions and chartered the Central Bank of Georgia and operated it with state funds.[13] Influenced by the new, rapid growth other businesses became necessary, including the construction of hotels, such as the Kimball House in 1871, and the establishment of many other small businesses, including Beck & Gregg Hardware Company and W. A. Moore, E.W. Marsh & Co., one of the many dry goods stores. By 1870 this wholesale dry goods firm reported sales of more than $1 million.[14] Another indication of the growth of Atlanta's population was the increase of saloons, which reached forty-five in 1876.[15] Rebuilding was remarkably quick, and many who had witnessed the state of Atlanta immediately following the war found the comeback to be phenomenal.

A group of enterprising businessmen, who through their success later became Atlanta's new elite, gained this position in the economic, civic, and political life of Atlanta because of the disruption caused by the Civil War. Atlanta was different from other Southern cities because the war had displaced most of its upper class. Coming to the city, the new businessmen had hopes of rebuilding it as well as their fortunes and lives. The Inman family, the topic of this study, is an example of people displaced by the war who became successful businessmen and civic leaders in the following decades. Many historians identify the Inmans as a founding family of Atlanta, closely tied to Atlanta's growth and development. The term "founding families" could encompass any family that had participated in business in Atlanta prior to the Civil War. Often "founding families" are also considered to be those who arrived after the war and who helped rebuild the city, a second kind of founding family. This term is similar to the confusing and vague "New South" term debated in the following pages. The family's success in the economic sector opened the way to prominent positions in the economic, civic, and political life of the city. An examination of the Inman family from Reconstruction through World War I and of its members' political, economical, and social roles will show how they helped shape Atlanta into the city it later became.

Soon the city was growing as rapidly as it had before the war. It was not long before the population reached its prewar high, and many businesses that had been successful before the war returned in large numbers. Now, however, many of these businesses had new owners. Most of the businessmen who came to Atlanta following the war were rural Southerners, and the majority of them had been somewhere between plantation owner and farmer of the middle class, sometimes referred to as a yeomen farmer. There were a few who were members of the plantation class and former Confederate soldiers, usually of the cavalry, and they all had lost economically in the war. Many had lost their homes, and all had lost their slaves, whose help was necessary in making a plantation profitable. Coming to Atlanta from the rural areas, they had hopes of recovering their families' losses and more. Along with the rural Southerners came Northerners who also saw Atlanta as a place of opportunity. Northerners who traveled South after the war in hopes of prospering in the economic situation did much toward the rebuilding of Atlanta during the Reconstruction period. These carpetbaggers had the financial means to buy large amounts of land in the South, which later gave them control of much of the best timberland in the region.[16] C. Vann Woodward noted that it was the initial purchases of land by these carpetbaggers that led to the influx of Northern capital, which the South so desperately needed at the end of the war. Once Northern capital began to make its way into the economy of the South, the rebuilding process was underway. The political Reconstruction imposed by the federal government may not have been entirely successful; however, it was the influx of Northern capital that was the source of Reconstruction, which revitalized the South. The Northern capital was not alone because there was also foreign capital, which aided in the recovery and rebuilding of the South.[17]

In many ways the city had simply picked up where it had been when the war began, and it appears that the war had merely been a period of lull in the history of an otherwise rapidly growing city. Historians have attempted to examine the South and its cities in order to address the issue of whether the New South, which refers the Southern United States in the decades following Reconstruction, was actually new or simply a continuation of the old. Each historian has approached the controversy from a different angle and has focused on various phases of Southern history. Those contemporary to this period believed that the South was undergoing many, often radical, changes that would make it economically, politically, and culturally competitive with the cities of the North, being different from the South prior to the Civil War, therefore "new." Men came to Atlanta, as they did to other Southern cities, and many had new ideas for how they could help the city prosper. The majority of those in political and economic power after the war were of some standing previous to the war. With these new men working with many of the old elites, there were many things that remained much the same. In the end the New South was not simply a continuation of the old with the old elite not being in direct control following Reconstruction. It was not new either, but was simply the old South picked up and dusted off a little, often with the sons of the former leaders taking control and giving a new face to the existing order.

C. Vann Woodward, the most influential historian of this period, detected several discontinuities between the old and the new South. According to Woodward, there were major dividing lines in politics and economics, and one of these was the Civil War. Those leading Atlanta after 1865 were not the same people they had been prior to the war, and Woodward believes that the leaders of politics in the new South were a new set of men with new ideas. These new men who led the way, according to Woodward, had come from outside the planter class, therefore being new, non-elites. The old planter regime he sees as having been severely crippled, if not destroyed entirely, and he also believes, along with the downfall of these old rulers was the collapse of "the leading financial, commercial, and industrial families of the region."[18] Laurence Shore, a historian predating Woodward, also felt these leaders were "discredited along with Lost Cause,"[19] thus signifying the fall of the old ruling class, leading to the establishment of a new group of leaders. Woodward does note a few exceptions to this theory of new men, such as Governor Joseph E. Brown, whose political power continued in spite of the war. Even though there were a few old names that appeared prior to and after the war that remained prominent and were among the new leaders, Woodward feels that it was not a return of the old system nor was the old ruling class restored, hence, a "New South."

Jonathan M. Wiener sees the planter class as being the political and economic leaders, and he emphasizes that this group of people were not new to these roles. Instead of a new South, Wiener recognizes the period after the Civil War as a continuation of the preceding period with elites of the plantations coming to the cities to be political and economic leaders.[20] They were new to the political and economic spheres but not non-elites. Other historians, including Dwight B. Billings and Paul Escott, agree with each other on the theory of continuity.[21] However, there are differences among historians regarding this. Wiener feels that the prominent antebellum leaders tried to destroy industry in the South following the war, and he uses Birmingham as an example of this.[22] Escott sees the prominent antebellum planters as the creators of the textile mills who helped revive industry in the South.[23] James Michael Russell agrees that the antebellum leaders survived the war and renewed their urban involvements. He disagrees with Woodward in believing that a middle class had been in existence before the war. Russell also sees the prewar and postwar elites as having few ties to the planter class.[24]

Laurence Shore finds that experienced ideologists and politicians, reasserting their influence after the war, were willing to make many changes in their ideology and rhetoric in order to remain in power.[25] This change in rhetoric was to adopt Northern terminology for labor, success, and economic development. In this line of thinking, the New South had its roots in the old and was only as new as necessary. Shore points out that many former antebellum political leaders served in postbellum positions and others were former plantation owners and their sons. This does not indicate that there was a tightly knit group of antebellum elites controlling the politics and economics of Georgia, but it does show that several of the postbellum leaders were of the same class as the prewar leaders. "But the most influential political leaders and shapers of public opinion in the postbellum period, 1865–1885, had held similar positions before and during the war. In the new politics, as in the new economics, ruling whites continued to rule."[26] This statement does not necessarily contradict Woodward, who admits that there were some postbellum leaders who had been in political positions previous to the war. The question between these two historians rides on the definition one uses for "new" and what percentage of leaders one would wish to use as the determining point between new and continuation of the old. Shore likes to approach the question by naming antebellum politicians or spokesmen who returned to politics following Reconstruction. Those in power after Reconstruction, whom Woodward calls Redeemers, were not all "new men," but a number were new to politics if not necessarily new to economic success. Although many of these men were from the plantation class, often they were the sons and had not been the owners.

When the war ended, many of those who were able to compete were those who had been competing economically and politically before the war. They perhaps did not have the same influence as they previously had, but they were leaders in the community. Those who once had money and status were able to use their previous knowledge, experiences, and contacts to further themselves after the war. Percentage wise it is evident that former governors and other political leaders may have taken a backseat during the Federal Reconstruction period. However, they were never far from political leadership. When it was possible for them to return to power, they returned with the blessings of the masses, whom, if nothing else, recognized their names from the prewar campaigns and enjoyed the familiarity. This same name recognition also played in the favor of many businessmen and their sons. After all, there is no substitute for a good name.

Those lesser-known individuals who were plantation owners from more rural areas benefited from their Confederate veteran status and their contacts with other better known, former elites. Therefore, the war may have simply opened the door to political, economic, and social success to lesser-known individuals, who were not necessarily less successful economically.

It is here that the Inmans fit, being of the plantation class of eastern Tennessee but not being politicians or members of the elites of Atlanta or any Southern city. The Civil War changed the status and the roles of several members of the Inman family. Shadrach W. Inman is an example of those plantation owners across the southeast that, having lost their previous way of living and their wealth, turned to business in order to rebuild their fortunes. Exactly how much wealth the Inmans had before the Civil War and how much they lost during the war is undetermined. Correct records of this type of information have been difficult to ascertain. Obviously, they lost their plantation lifestyle and their antebellum livelihood even if they did have funds invested in Northern or English banks. Shadrach's brothers, William H. Inman and Walker P. Inman, are models of prewar businessmen who returned to business, but not necessarily to the same business in which they had engaged before the war. William went to New York near the end of the war, and Walker remained in Atlanta, fleeing to Augusta when Atlanta fell. Samuel M. Inman and John H. Inman, the two eldest sons of Shadrach, demonstrated the success of Confederate soldiers and sons of a planter who were able to put the war behind them and to prosper to the point of becoming two of the wealthiest men on the east coast, according to contemporary reports. Samuel, being the eldest son, also had the benefits of an extensive education and was a student at Princeton University when the Civil War began, a luxury afforded to few Southern elites. Hugh T. Inman, the youngest son of Shadrach, demonstrated the usage of family ties and contacts, and the ability to invest in various industries while they were in their early stages. The investing in numerous young industries is perhaps the most dominant family characteristic of the Inmans in the years immediately following the Civil War. These men of the plantation class were able to regain their wealth and increase it due to connections they had established before the war and because of their experience in business. However, whether these opportunities existed for men who had creative ideas and courage but lacked the professional and social contacts is hard to determine, although it is probable that one also needed connections to prosper as well. The Inmans' ability to build a number of successful companies led to their becoming prominent in this new society; their connections with other businessmen whom they knew from before the war and their prewar experience in merchandising and plantation management led to their becoming part of the elite in the New South. This idea is informed by the work of Don H. Doyle with the Inman family serving as an example of Doyle's theory that Atlanta was a city which, not having an entrenched upper class following the war, was open to people migrating to the city with the hopes of creating new lives for themselves and their families, and in the process, creating new cities.[27] This creation of new cities was the establishing of such things as new businesses, improved industries, new political leaders, and new social clubs.

Doyle presents an account of the new men who came to build the new cities that ultimately was the New South. Doyle does note that few of Atlanta's leading men in 1880 were young. The average birth date was 1827, and a large number of these had arrived in Atlanta before the war began with 26 percent of 1880 elite in Atlanta appearing in the 1860 City Directory and 38 percent of 1880 elite arriving before 1861. Newcomers were denoted as those arriving after 1865, coming from the rural areas of Georgia and east Tennessee, and being pro-Southern although few were actually veterans.[28]

The connections between the success of the city and the personal success of the individual businessmen are a major driving point for the booster spirit, according to Doyle. It was this spirit that created a powerful, adhesive business class.[29] An obvious tie is in the rise and fall of real estate values. It was real estate that the local businessmen treated as an investment. These men helped build the city putting in place such infrastructures as water works and sewer systems and also serving as public officials. They supported the city growth by constructing their own buildings, such as hotels and financial institutions. Most diversified their investments across a wide spectrum of businesses, giving themselves many advantages.

The Inman family is used in this study as a supporting example of Don Doyle's new men, coming into Atlanta and creating a new city. Not only do the Inman's fit the description of the migrants arriving just before the war, as Sam and Walker did, and they acquired the rank of elite in roughly fifteen years, but they also served as city builders and boosters on many different levels. Even in Doyle's description of these new elites he noted that often-exaggerated hardships were very typical "in the self-congratulatory, often highly sentimental life of American men of wealth in the nineteenth century."[30] And the Inman's meet this description as well. The privileges and wealth they possessed were played down and their setbacks were emphasized. If there was any major problem with conducting this research, those glowing depictions were it. It has been all but impossible to get around. Even when desiring to show the Inmans in their true light, the only records that research uncovers support the praising accounts that ran in the local newspapers of the day or appeared in the occasional dedication pamphlet written for the purpose of praise. Although every attempt has been made to give the reader an unbiased view of the Inman's, the truth is that all that can be reported is what the research supports. Obviously, any less than level dealings or any unethical business practices were not recorded in the records that have survived. The reader should simply keep these factors in mind as they read the glorifying reviews. If nothing else, these reviews also serve as support to Doyle's theory.

After becoming economic leaders of Atlanta in the 1870s, the Inmans were responsible for numerous improvements and changes in the city. They were instrumental in advancing higher education in Atlanta and served as trustees on boards of several colleges. Local politics and civic duties received much of their attention, and they sponsored cultural activities in the city, a reflection of their many trips to New York and Europe. Transforming the city into a prosperous economic center for the South and embracing its cultural life were the goals of the Inman family. Its members were active boosters of Atlanta, for if a man's home city was prosperous, then it reflected nicely on him and his business. Not only did their business success depend on Atlanta's being a successful industrial and economic center, but most of the Atlanta businessmen had large real estate investments, which they hoped would rise in value.[31] It was this process of city building that made the local businessmen a separate class and demonstrated their common interest in promoting Atlanta.[32] Many of the businessmen felt that the promotion of Atlanta was their job.[33] The desire to make Atlanta the leading city in the South was common among all whom had invested time and energy in the area. This led to the development and strong support for the Chamber of Commerce and similar organizations, which strove to keep Atlanta growing. Never did the boosters question the effects of the rapid growth of the city and the social problems that followed. Beyond the average businessman, boosterism enlisted the aid of the local and state governments as well as newspaper editors and propagandists.[34] Henry W. Grady, perhaps the most notable and vocal booster of the South, concerned himself with the promotion of Atlanta and not the South as a whole.[35] But if there were any carry-over benefits to the region, he would not complain, and this sentiment was typical of the boosters of Atlanta. Boosterism was successful if the objectives were local and clearly defined. Atlanta was the place of opportunity for the Inman family, and it was an opportunity that they took full advantage of.

The Inman family came to Atlanta from Dandridge, Tennessee, which is the second oldest town in that state. Abednego Inman, born 1 July 1752, had married Mary Ritchie, a woman from Wales, in 1777, and the couple soon came to America from England following his two older brothers, Shadrach and Meshach.[36] A member of the Continental forces, Shadrach died at Musgrove's Mill on 19 August 1780; Indians killed his brother, Meshach, while he was exploring the Cumberland Mountains. Abednego was among the earliest settlers of Jefferson County, Tennessee, where he was the justice of the peace.[37] The couple had a son named John Ritchie Inman, who married Jane Walker and had a son named Shadrach "Shade" Walker Inman, born 17 September 1811, in Dandridge.[38] Shadrach grew up in Dandridge, but the family moved to Madison County, Alabama, near present day Huntsville, after the three eldest children died in a house fire. Shadrach remained in Alabama until the age of twenty-five, when he returned to Dandridge to live with his grandfather and to engage in bartering goods and trading cotton around Douglas Lake and along its tributaries, the French Broad, the Nolichucky, and the Lick rivers.

It was by means of his boats that Shadrach was able to engage in various types of trade. Country storekeepers were the most important Southern middlemen in various types of businesses, including the cotton trade. In the antebellum period most people had only a few bales of cotton and did not have enough to send to a factor. However, the small storekeepers in the rural areas would accept cotton as payment for dry goods. In turn the storekeeper, acting as a factor, would send his collected set of bales to an agency in his own name.[39] This appears to be what Shadrach did. Doing more than the typical storekeeper, he went out into the rural areas on his boat carrying goods and bartering for cotton and other produce. He continued to run the dry goods store as well where his brother, Walker, learned the business by helping him. Shadrach had been responsible for raising Walker and William after their parents died while they were still young. Shadrach's ability to travel through the area on flat-boats, which he used to carry his goods, and the many connections he had developed made it possible for him to trade in slaves as well.[40]

Shadrach was successful in his bartering of goods, and he became a rather powerful man in the Dandridge community. By the time of the Civil War, he was a wealthy plantation owner, a successful merchant, and a public figure in the town. Shadrach's estate was estimated to be worth $100,000 according to his obituary written not quite thirty years later.[41] The Inman plantation was between two and three miles square,[42] and it contained a large gristmill, a sawmill, and a row of slave cabins.[43] Much of the prewar information on the Inmans, particularly Shadrach, was gathered years after the fact from the biased memories of family members and friends. Much of this information comes from oral interviews conducted by Evelyn Yates Inman, the wife of Arthur Crew Inman, Sam's grandson. Evelyn conducted the interviews during the fall of 1926 and the winter and spring of 1927 to enable Arthur to write his book, *The Inman Diary: A Public & Private Confession*, edited by Daniel Aaron.[44] Obviously, these testaments of his worth and moral standing should be viewed with the highest level of scrutiny.

Many of the Inmans' neighbors were unionists, a characteristic of many eastern Tennesseans at the time. Since the Inman family supported the Confederacy, having Sam and John in the CSA cavalry, they report-edly suffered at their neighbors' hands during the war. Family legend was that the women would wear two or three dresses at a time to keep them from being destroyed by Northern troops or by other unionist sympa-thizers who frequently appeared at the Inman home. In the piano they hid their other dresses, and in the large hoops they pinned valuables for safekeeping. The Inmans' slave, Aunt Dicy, told that she made a bed with a layer of meat in it, and she slept on it every night beginning sometime during the second year of the war in order to keep it from being stolen. Much of the Inmans' personal property, including the gristmill, the Federal soldiers destroyed.[45] Even after the war ended, the home guards shot at Shadrach while he rode on his plantation, and the family moved to town in hopes of finding security. Eventually, they also gave up their store when the Federal soldiers returned repeatedly to harass them and to loot their stock according to their former slave, Aunt Dicy.[46] Soon after the war ended Shadrach decided to move his family to Atlanta where they would be safe.[47]

Shadrach was not the first Inman to move to Atlanta, since his younger brother, Walker Patterson Inman, had arrived there in 1859 as an agent for the Northwestern Bank of Georgia in Ringgold, joining his brother, William H. Inman.[48] The earliest indication that Walker was in Atlanta was when he and his wife joined the First Presbyterian Church of Atlanta by certificate on 17 November 1861.[49] Walker also appears on the Fulton County Tax Digest, 1861 as being a resident of Atlanta and owning real estate valued at $2,000, two slaves valued at $1,500, and $600 in other property.[50] This tax digest also lists him as an agent for North Western Bank, paying $200 in taxes for the bank. Early in the Civil War, Walker had served in the cavalry, but a throw from his horse and an injury to his back shortened his military career. He returned to banking in Atlanta and continued in the business through the war. His other interests included the wholesale house of Inman, Cole and Company, located in the Franklin Building on Alabama Street, which specialized in dry goods including sundry pastries according to the county taxes, and he served as an agent for this company. The company appears to have been doing very well. Its total value in 1864 was $53,600. In this business Walker worked as a commission merchant and sold flour, corn, corn whiskey, rye whiskey, tobacco and sugar.[51] The company also sold lots of land in many Georgia counties.[52] Throughout most of the war, Walker and his family stayed in Atlanta, although during the Union Army's siege of the city they fled to Augusta. After the war, Walker and his family chose to remain in Augusta because fire had destroyed their home in Atlanta along with their business. Before the war, Walker's personal property in Fulton County had totaled $64,500.[53] Walker established and ran a dry goods store in Augusta; where he got the money to open this dry goods store is unclear, but rumor was that he had a bale of cotton that he sold at the end of the war. It is interesting that he chose to remain in Augusta. This may have been because the cotton market in Augusta, like many of the port cities, was able to commence trading cotton quickly.

Shadrach W. Inman came to Atlanta in 1865, joining the First Presbyterian Church of Atlanta on 2 December 1865, along with his wife, Katherine Ann Lee, and his three youngest children, Martha Ella, Sara Emma, and Shadrach Lee,and immediately set up a dry goods store on the corner of Marietta and Whitehall streets.[54] Diagonally across the street, he secured his son, Hugh, in another dry goods store. The question of how Shadrach was able to set up two dry goods stores so soon after leaving Dandridge is not determined. It is possible that he had been able to store away cotton during the war but would have had to hide it from his neighbors as well as the Northern soldiers. Cotton saved during the war was a tremendous investment because it was in such high demand in the North in 1865. Cotton had been king before the war, and cotton continued its reign immediately following it. There is the possibility that Shadrach was able to continue to trade cotton during the war and sell goods, which came through the blockade. Since his brother, William, was in New York with the cotton trade, perhaps he had an arrangement or was able to receive a loan of much needed Northern capital. There is also the possibility that the Inmans had invested their money in the Northern or English banks previous to the war, providing them with the cash necessary for so many capitalistic endeavors. Whatever the case, Shadrach was able to come to Atlanta with his family and open two new stores. The establishment of stores does not appear to be that unusual. During the war Southerners had done without many material goods, and there was such a demand for goods that "when the war ended, there was a rush into the storekeeping business."[55] It was not long before Shadrach was trading in cotton on a larger scale than before the war.

After the Civil War ended in 1865, Samuel Martin Inman, the eldest son of Shadrach, went to Augusta, where he worked under the guidance of his uncle, Walker P. Inman, in Walker's dry goods store. Joined by Sam's friend and future brother-in-law, Samuel K. Dick, the three began to engage in the trading of cotton.[56] Here again was the mixture of dry goods and cotton trading that seems to have been very beneficial to the Inman family. John H. Inman, Shadrach's second son, went to New York

City to join his uncle, William H. Inman, to start in the cotton trade there. William does show up on the Fulton County Tax Records as having moved to Atlanta by 1864, and his total property value in Fulton County was $79,600.[57] He fled Atlanta during the war to an unknown destination and is known to have been in New York by 1865. Under various names their company acted as a partner firm of the Inmans' Atlanta cotton trading firms. Many Southern firms had partners in New York, finding it beneficial to have someone close to the market and the exchange.[58]

In 1867, the cotton business in Augusta was growing rapidly, and Atlanta was beginning to recover from the Civil War. Once again, the railroads were running and the advantage they provided a company should not be underestimated. Speculating in cotton was proving to be profitable again, if one had the money necessary for this type of activity. The high price of cotton after the war and the possibility of immediate profit encouraged many people to establish themselves as cotton merchants.[59] Not only were individuals getting involved, but many banks as well felt that speculating in cotton was a risk, which promised high returns. Walker and Sam decided that their business would benefit from the rails leading to Atlanta and from an association with Shadrach. Walker and Sam relocated to Atlanta, and the office in Augusta became a branch and remained so through numerous changes in the business. Shadrach put all of his time and money into the cotton company named S. W. Inman & Son. This business appears to have existed previous to Shadrach's moving to Atlanta because in 1864 the Fulton County tax records listed Samuel M. Inman as agent for it. The business name did not appear on the taxes again until 1867, but the early mention of the business indicates that Shadrach had been trading in cotton during the war. With the reappearance of S. W. Inman & Son in 1867, the family members formed a network for buying and selling cotton. Walker became the financial watcher of S. W. Inman & Son, and Shadrach and Samuel acted as the buyers in these early years. It was a big success almost instantly because it faced no real competition in Atlanta at this time. In

1867, S. W. Inman & Son handled approximately 1,500 bales. This was the beginning of the rebuilding of the Inmans' fortunes.

The Inmans' role in the cotton trade was neither that of farmers who grew the product nor that of factory owners who needed it to produce a product that they sold for their livelihood. The Inmans were middlemen who were financing and marketing the crop, and until recently this particular role in the cotton industry was overlooked. The role of factors and agents will be further discussed in chapter 1.

Because the Inmans first focused on establishing their businesses and since it was due to the success of these, which enabled them to enlarge their areas of interest, the first chapter of this study will focus on their businesses. The importance of the businesses in setting the Inmans as elites should not be overlooked. It was this success, therefore, which enabled them to participate in political, civic, and social arenas. Once their wealth was established, they had more time to participate in politics, becoming active advocates of the boosterism of Atlanta. Their financial success also gave them the means to support various civic and cultural causes and address race issues. Since the Inman women, typical of women of the late nineteenth century, did not play a visibly active role in the family's businesses, the part they played does not become fully evident until the civic life and social culture is examined. And even in these areas their roles are perhaps understated. However, this study examines documented roles of each member of the family, leaving the reader to determine for themselves the roles of the female members of the Inman family. One should be aware, however, that it was not desirable for a woman of an elite social status to have her name appear in the local newspaper beyond such topics as dinners held and guests entertained. As the old saying goes, the name of a woman of good breeding should appear in the newspaper paper only twice, once when she gets married and once when she dies. Although that may be extreme, it does demonstrate the role women of a particular social status were to have acknowledged publicly.

Along with the many changes that the Civil War caused, there were a number of things that did not change. These were somewhat imbedded into the social and economic fabric of the South such as cotton, the prewar favorite crop, which returned to power throughout the South. It was cotton that led the South back into the national and international economy until other crops and industries could be established; and as elements of the old South returned, Atlanta began to grow again and with it new businesses began to prosper as well. Looking back with population numbers and business records, the Civil War appears as a brief interruption in the otherwise fast-paced growth of Atlanta. Much of the city's growth and revitalization was due to the migration of Southerners from the rural areas, who had fought for the Confederacy and were proud of the fact. Typically these new Atlantans from the rural South owned the new, prospering businesses, and the war had not diminished their loyalty to the South but had simply strengthened it. As businessmen they faced the reality that to restore the South to prosperity they would have to compete with the North in industrial production. Using Northern capital as backing was essential to competition, and to gain it required business relationships and cordial friendships. So businessmen put aside their differences in the name of economic cooperation, and new entrepreneurs had no problem in doing business with Northern investors who had much needed capital. Cotton once again took a commanding position in the economy of the area and the production of cotton was on the increase. This was the Atlanta the Inmans found when they arrived in the city immediately following the war.

1

THE INMAN FAMILY'S BUSINESSES:
King Cotton and the Railroads

COTTON MAY NOT HAVE RETURNED TO THE STATUS OF "KING" AFTER the Civil War, but there was still a substantial amount of money to be made in the business. Farmers throughout the South grew cotton as their cash crop, and the industries in the North and in Europe persisted in demanding it. Getting cotton from the fields to the factories was where fortunes could be made. Middlemen purchased various grades of cotton from farmers throughout the South and had it compressed, allowing the cotton to be shipped in a space significantly smaller than unpressed bales. This made it more economical to ship cotton, saving the middlemen money in shipping charges. The selling of cotton to Northern factories at a price greater than it was bought from the Southern farmers was called cotton brokeraging. These brokers or middlemen Harold D. Woodman refers to as king cotton's retainers because they promoted cotton through financing and marketing, enabling it to retain its importance in the world economy.[60] These "retainers" were factors or agents for cotton firms, which were based in market areas or transportation hubs and found it advantageous to have agents in port cities in order to store the cotton and ship it by freighter at first notice. Cotton factors during the antebellum period would loan money to cotton farmers, purchase supplies for the plantation, secure credit when needed, receive cotton from same farmers, house it, insure it, and send it to the market where and when it would get the best price. A major characteristic of the factor was his empowerment to transact business for the farmer, or more correctly the plantation owner, and his freedom to deal using his own discretion. The factors actively pursued cotton, going into the interior visiting planters and small farmers hoping to represent them in the cotton market. In return a factor received a percentage of the sale, approximately 2.5 percent on average. The farmer reimbursed the factor the cost of shipping, housing and insuring the cotton, as well as for any advances made for supplies and living expenses received from the factor. Many agencies employed both factors and brokers.[61] Factors differed from cotton brokers in that brokers graded cotton and this gave them substantial power over the cotton trade. Factors simply sold cotton for a percentage while brokers would buy for a company and then resale for a profit. Factors had much more personal contact with the farmer and received the trust of that individual. Their relationship would continue throughout the year where as the relationship with the broker would have been just once a year, during the cotton selling season. In the years immediately following the war, the role of factor decreased and the role of broker increased drastically. Bypassing factors, farmers and itinerant merchants, who held cotton in trade for store goods, began to deal directly with the banks and manufacturers. They also began to deal directly with the brokers themselves, who represented their employing cotton firm which would buy the cotton from the farmer and then sell it at the greatest profit they could. Often this meant holding on the cotton for a period of time until a better price was being paid. However, large firms continued to act as factors for many of their more important clients, providing them with many services.

Next to factors the storekeepers during the antebellum period were the most important Southern middlemen in the cotton trade. Less the personal business manager than the factor, they still provided much of the same services upon request. In addition to selling the crop, they also provided credit and dealt with the smaller farmers who may not even have a full bale of cotton. These smaller growers would have fell through the system under the factors. However, the storekeepers were not parallel to the factors. Instead, the storekeepers usually became a customer of a factor after collecting the cotton in place of money owed him for supplies advanced the previous growing season. Itinerant merchants took the role of storekeeper a step further, peddling their wares over the countryside and collecting cotton in payment. This was the type of storekeeping Shadrach W. Inman had conducted in eastern Tennessee prior to the Civil War.

The Inmans' primary business was in cotton brokeraging and in cotton futures, but their interests included manufacturing cotton textiles, steel hoops for holding compressed cotton and other cotton related items. Beyond the cotton industry, the Inmans, as diverse businessmen, also had an interest in Atlanta real estate, wholesale dry goods, insurance, railroads, streetcars, and banking. These other interests may appear to be greatly different from the brokeraging and marketing of cotton, but upon closer examination one understands these businesses' connections to cotton. Cotton was the center of the South's economy, and it was the center of the family's financial strategies. Most of the other businesses in which they were involved were for the support of or were directly related to the cotton industry and other businesses evolved from them.

Dry goods stores were the pivotal point on which the crops got to market and the farmers obtained goods. In a speech to small merchants, Henry W. Grady praised small country stores as being a more important institution to the cotton industry than factors.[62] The country store, referred to in this study as itinerant merchants, provided the small farmers with necessities such as seeds and general household goods, first in a bartering system and later on credit. As the cotton business grew, the necessity of a storefront faded as farmers began to skip the itinerant merchants, receiving credit from banks instead, and deal directly with brokers in firms they selected.

Brokers received cotton from the factors, and factors received cotton from planters and from itinerant merchants who collected cotton from small farmers who came into the dry goods stores. Instead of receiving money for their cotton immediately, the farmer waited for the factor to get the cotton to a broker in a port city who in turn would ship the cotton to the market, hoping for the highest price possible. Only after the cotton sold and the factor received handling fees would the farmer get his money. Between the harvest and the sale were often several months during which time the farmer needed farming supplies and household items. Often factors would hold cotton hoping for a better price or hoping to make one large shipment of cotton consisting of the crops of many local farmers. The factor would forward the farmer any supplies he needed while the cotton was on the way to the market. After the cotton sold, the factor would give the farmer his money minus the cost of any materials he had been given on credit.

Although the Inmans ran a dry goods store, they originally were involved in bartering dry goods for cotton up and down the rivers on flat-boats. They would send the cotton to a factor that was in charge of selling it at the best price. This active pursuit of cotton technically makes the early Inmans itinerant merchants engaging in the early stages of the cotton trade. After the war, family members were living in Atlanta, Augusta, and New York. Those in New York immediately called their business a cotton agency, but those in Atlanta and Augusta continued to run dry goods stores, which could be seen as places that small farmers came into to trade cotton for goods and could receive credit on future cotton crops for supplies.

Where the Inmans got the money necessary to start over, particularly with two dry goods stores in Atlanta and one in Augusta and a cotton agency in New York, is not known. It is possible that the Inmans had been able to hide bales of cotton from the Union troops and Union sympathizers during the war. With the new dry goods stores, the Inmans were able to remain open to a large community of people who brought their cotton to sell. Chances are that the Inmans also acted as peddling itinerant merchants, going out into the surrounding country searching for cotton, but soon most producers of the crop brought it directly to Atlanta for sale.

As work began to pick up, many of the itinerant merchants like the Inmans dropped the stores, but retained their port city contacts and brokers. These port cities served as branches to the central business, which was in an area newly rich in cotton, the piedmont of Georgia. Atlanta was the perfect interior location because of its railroads. Before Atlanta developed as a center of the cotton trade, Augusta was an important cotton port because of its unique location, within reach of the piedmont of Georgia but still with access to the Atlantic Ocean via the Savannah River. Savannah became the most important port city in the area when the Central of Georgia Railroad was repaired following the war.

Shadrach's business, S. W. Inman & Son, flourished, and the family began to build a wealth equivalent to what they had enjoyed before the war. After officially moving the family to Atlanta, the Inmans achieved considerable prosperity, as indicated by the tax records of Fulton County. The earliest record of the Inmans in Atlanta was Sam being listed on the 1863 Fulton County Tax Records as an agent, another term for broker, for S. W. Inman and Son. This indicates that S. W. Inman & Son existed before the Civil War ended and that Shadrach was already beginning to move from the role of itinerant merchant to cotton firm with factors. However, there is no real indication of how the business was doing, particularly with the cotton blockades in place. Also during this time Sam was serving in the Confederate Army and this limited the time he spent as a factor in Atlanta during the war.

Soon after the war the transition was not complete, but the Inmans were using both the itinerant merchant system and the factor system to establish themselves economically. Shadrach's personal property in Fulton County in 1869 was worth $20,950. By 1869, Sam had been working full-time as an agent, or broker, for the company for two years, and the value of his personal property in the city was $8,000 and his other property totaled $1,600. In 1870, with the cotton business well established and prospering, Shadrach retired and moved back to the old family home in Dandridge, Tennessee. Sam took over the business, changing the name to S. M. Inman & Company.

At the insistence of his sons, Shadrach returned to Atlanta in the mid–1870s. He retained an office in S. M. Inman & Company for the remainder of his life. Many felt that Sam liked to keep Shadrach around to make him feel like he was helping in business matters. Shadrach was remembered by those who visited the office as the hand-shaker and the one who entertained the customers.

It is in 1870 that the first real post war economic numbers for Atlanta were gathered. In 1870, 117 individuals, who constituted 1 percent of the population over the age of 21, owned 55 percent of Atlanta's wealth.[63] This percentage not only shows the disparity of wealth in the general population of Atlanta, but it also demonstrates the status and wealth the Inmans had achieved in a short period of time. It was being members of this small group of people that entitled the Inmans to the status of elites.

By 1878, S. M. Inman & Company was handling 45,000 bales annually, and in four years the company reached the magic number of 100,000 bales, and they opened an office in Houston, Texas. By 1890, the company was in charge of 225,000 bales.[64] By 1890, the number of businesses in Atlanta had increased dramatically: 46 wholesale and retail dry goods firms, 9 wholesale and retail hardware houses, and 28 wholesale and retail grocery businesses, with cotton falling in the dry goods category.

In 1891, with the firm handling half a million bales of cotton, worth $20 million dollars annually,[65] and employing over five hundred people, the *Atlanta Constitution* announced that S. M. Inman & Company was the largest cotton house in the world. It was in the same newspaper article that the Inman family of Atlanta was estimated to be worth $15 million demonstrating the economic growth of which they were part.[66]

This increase in bales reflected the increase of production of cotton by the upcountry cotton farmers who took advantage of Atlanta's marketing and processing facilities and of the opening up of the Texas cotton frontier and the Mississippi.[67] In 1867 there were only 17,000 bales of cotton coming into Atlanta; this number grew to almost 76,000 in 1876, but by 1880 the number had risen to 107,223 and then to 120,000 in 1886.[68] Much of this increase of cotton through Atlanta reflected greater production after the war, but the rebuilding and expansion and the improvement of the railway system and a common gauge also contributed to it. After railroad gauges were standardized between the North and the South in 1886, the number of cotton bales shipped from Atlanta grew and in 1890 totaled 270,000. Atlanta had four large cotton warehouses and several firms with national and international connections by 1880. The largest of these was S. M. Inman and Company,[69] and many considered Sam to be the "leading force behind the Atlanta cotton trade."[70]

Along with the growth came more branch offices for S. M. Inman and Company around the Southern United States and Europe, including Savannah, Georgia, Houston, Texas, New York, and one in Bremen, Germany.[71] Part of Sam Inman's success in the cotton business was that he helped farmers by grading their cotton and insuring it for no charge. This was considered by those in the cotton business as a major consideration, saving millions of dollars for the farmers.[72]

S. M. Inman & Company was a strong company, which continued to grow and gain respect across the South. Not only was it important to Atlanta for its reputation as the largest cotton house in the world, but also the company's employment of a large number of people, which totaled five hundred in 1892. Local newspapers proclaimed that cotton markets across the United States felt the company's power. In the summer of 1888, cotton prices suffered greatly and there was a panic in the industry. Legend is that S. M. Inman & Company helped stop the panic by getting behind the market at what appeared to local businessmen and journalists to have been the crucial moment. Many powerful cotton houses and speculators went out of business during this economic crisis, but S. M. Inman & Company survived and retained the confidence of the many sellers in the South and buyers in the North.[73] However, although the *Atlanta Constitution* printed the above with a list of glowing adjectives, there is no evidence supporting the rumor that S. M. Inman & Company actually stopped the market panic. This is just another example of glowing stories published in the local newspapers.

The Inman family's interest in cotton was not limited to the South nor to the family members living in Atlanta. John H. Inman, Shadrach's second son, had interests similar to those of his father, his uncles, and his brothers, but he felt that he could personally prosper better in New York City. When asked why he chose to go to New York, he pointed to the destitute state of the South following the war. Some family friends felt that Shadrach sent John to help William H. Inman, Shadrach's brother, or at least to keep an eye on his business dealings. John went to New York after the war and joined William, who was working as a Wall Street banker.[74] John worked with his uncle as a cashier for a few years as well as with S. W. Inman & Company, serving as the company's New York connection. Along with Alfred Austell, another displaced Southerner sympathizer from eastern Tennessee, William began the cotton firm of Austell, Inman & Company; and John H. Inman and James Swann, another Southerner sympathizer from eastern Tennessee and the son-in-law of Alfred Austell, served as clerks for the company. In the next few years, the company prospered and grew quickly, and by 1868 John Inman had become a full partner in the firm.[75] Alfred Austell and William H. Inman retired from active business in 1870, and the company became Inman, Swann & Company, housed in the Cotton Exchange Building in New York City, and under the ownership of John H. Inman and James Swann.[76] A firm with capital and influence, Inman, Swann & Company continued to act as factor for many large cotton speculators, including B. W. Heard of Washington County, Georgia, and its former owners, Alfred Austell of Atlanta and William H. Inman. As Heard's factor, the company sold his cotton, handled his bank statements, and even collected his railroad stock dividends. It was this total financial management and continued one-on-one service that the large cotton brokerage firms continued to supply their larger patrons.

As a member of the firm, John Inman helped organize the New York Cotton Exchange, which began trading on 7 September 1870, and was incorporated on 8 April 1871, by a special act of the New York legislature. Before the creation of the cotton exchange, the lack of a central meeting place forced brokers to go to various offices to make trades, often losing deals and missing buyers and sellers. To eliminate this problem, brokers began to congregate in the office of James F. Wenman and Company on Pearl Street in New York City in order to buy or sell cotton.[77] This was the beginning of the New York Cotton Exchange. It followed the establishment of the Liverpool exchange in 1869; the New Orleans Cotton Exchange appeared soon afterward.[78] The purpose of the exchange was to set a common grading scale for all cotton brokers to follow, making for fair-trading when they purchased cotton sight unseen. It also enabled agencies to deal in cotton futures, which served as contracts for particular grades of cotton to be delivered later and gave speculators new opportunities in the cotton market.[79] Brokers also hoped that the cotton exchange would give them the ability to control the amounts of certain grades of cotton grown and sent to market. John H. Inman served as one of the first members of the Board of Managers of the exchange,[80] and Inman, Swann & Company had representatives on the board until the 1920s.[81]

Inman, Swann & Company worked closely with S. M. Inman & Company just as Austell, Inman & Company had worked with S. W. Inman & Son. Sam bought the cotton from farmers in the South and sold it to John's company in New York, which in turn sold it to a production company or factory in the North or in Europe. If there was a particular grade of cotton for which a manufacturer was asking, John got Sam to find some and buy it even if it was in the off season. Sometimes they negotiated to sell cotton they had not yet bought, and these were the early dealings in cotton futures. When time came to buy the cotton, which they had already sold, sometimes the grade of cotton they had sold in futures would cost more than they had expected due to a shortage of supply or an increase in demand. The agencies also dealt in spot cotton, which is cotton that is available for immediate purchase, or available "on-the-spot." In order to conduct such an intricate business, Sam and John were in contact with each other on a daily basis, first by telegrams and letters, later by telephone. An example of the two organizations working together is in the account books of S. M. Inman & Company. In April 1883, Inman, Swann & Company of New York was listed in the ledger with accounts totaling $122,689.17.[82]

In 1867 Shadrach's third son, Hugh T. Inman, went to New York City to work as an office boy for Austell, Inman & Company. According to family members, he arrived there with twelve dollars in his pocket, and he borrowed money from his brother, John, to begin investing in cotton. John guided his cotton speculating, and soon Hugh had made $6,000.[83] The amount of money Hugh had when he arrived in New York is an unproven bit of family legend told by family members during an oral interview. If nothing else, this proves that stories of starting over with next-to-nothing were favored by the family and told with a sense of pride.

Hugh used this money to purchase an interest in Inman, Swann & Company, which was his employer after the retirement of Alfred Austell and William H. Inman. While he was still with the company, Inman, Swann & Company transferred Hugh to the Savannah, Georgia, branch where he ran the office and continued to add to his assets. In 1876, after amassing $200,000, Hugh retired from Inman, Swann & Company, feeling that cotton trading and speculating were too risky.[84] Part of Hugh's payoff from selling his shares was a lot of land on the corner of Peachtree and Harris streets. He moved with his family to Atlanta and built a large, Victorian-style brick house on this property. The family lived in this house until 1909, when they built a large stone house on West Peachtree Street across from the present day Biltmore Hotel.

Retiring from active business did not exclude one from continuing to speculate in cotton, as records indicate was the case with Alfred Austell and William H. Inman as well as Hugh T. Inman.[85] Although he was retired from active business, in 1883 the ledger books of S. M. Inman &

Company indicate that Hugh was still involved with the company, earning a salary of $250 and profiting from cotton trading frequently.

Hugh's main business in the years following his resignation from Inman, Swann & Company was the Exposition Cotton Mills in Atlanta, organized in 1882.[86] The Exposition Cotton Mills was the direct product of the International Cotton Exposition of 1881, which according to Harold D. Davis was Atlanta's awakening to the possibilities of the manufacturing of cotton.[87] This and the other expositions will be discussed in chapter 2 of this study.

After the expo, which was an act of city boosterism to benefit not only the city but specifically the cotton industry, twenty-five businessmen, including Hugh T. Inman, Walker P. Inman, James Swann, William W. Austell, son of the late Alfred Austell, and Samuel M. Inman, wanted another cotton mill added to Atlanta.[88] The others participating in the meeting to bring a new mill into Atlanta were many of the city's elites: Mayor James W. English, George W. Parrott, Frank P. Rice, Robert H. Richards, William B. Cox, Evan P. Howell, who was editor-in-chief of the *Atlanta Constitution*, James H. Porter, Thomas L. Langston, John L. Hopkins, Richard Peters and J. W. Murphy. The Exhibit Hall of the International Cotton Exposition was turned into the Exposition Cotton Mill.[89] The men put forth $10,000 each as financial support, and they elected Hugh as the company's first president.[90] There was an initial stock issue of $250,000, and Walker P. Inman acquired nearly one-third of the company's stock.[91] The petition was signed by most of the businessmen who attended the meeting with the mayor, and one important person who was not present at the meeting but who signed the petition for the Exposition Cotton Mill was James Swann.[92] This was a logical business decision considering the amount of cotton that was coming into Atlanta at the time. It was an immediate success and, according to one historian, "has had much to do with the growth of the cotton milling industry in the South."[93]

By 1890 the Exposition Cotton Mills had five hundred employees and had spun fifty million yards of yarn. Laborers received $1.00 daily in

1889, and a skilled worker could make between $1.25 and $3.50 a day. As was the case in many mills, most of the work force was women who earned from $1.50 to $10.00 for a six-day week, averaging eleven hours per day. As compensation for their low wages, cheap housing was offered to the workers. Monthly rentals for cottages at the Exposition Mill ranged from $2.50 to $4.00, and all 425 workers in 1888 lived there. Cotton mills in Atlanta were the major employers of white women and girls in the 1880s.[94]

A glance at the mill's account books demonstrates the magnitude of business the mill did and the influence it had on cotton in Atlanta. Of course, the Inmans appeared listed individually, as well as Inman, Swann & Company. Supplies the firm purchased from the Atlanta Woolen Ware Company, another Inman family business, paid the Georgia Institute of Technology at various times rather small amounts for what appear to have been repairs to the mill's equipment. Demonstrating the activity of the mill were the expense accounts, which listed picking, carding, spinning, spooling, weaving, drawing-in, slasher, cloth, boiler room and shop, and yard.[95] The mill obviously had a significant impact on the cotton industry in Atlanta, and the Inman family benefited greatly from it. Hugh T. Inman remained actively involved with the mill until his death in 1910.

Loosely connected to the Exposition Cotton Mill was the cotton press that Hugh T. Inman operated. The need to transport cotton fueled the desire to compress the cotton in order to bring the cost down as low as possible. The cotton press which the Inmans set up and operated was separate from the firm, making it possible for other agencies to use it. The press itself became a moneymaking investment because for many years it was the only one in the Atlanta area; it could press as many as four thousand bales a day.[96] After the cotton was pressed, steel rings or hoops were needed to keep the cotton in the compressed stage, so the Inmans invested in the Atlanta Steel Hoop Company. It is interesting to note that the Atlanta Steel Hoop Company, the city's first steel hoop mill, was not founded until 1901 by George Washington Conners. In 1906, the company's name was changed to Atlanta Steel Company, and in 1915 it became Atlantic Steel Company.[97]

Another of Hugh's business interests directly related to cotton was the clothing factory of Inman, Smith & Company. Founded by Hugh and run by his son, Edward, this company also proved to be a very profitable venture. The main product of the company was men's clothing. There were seven such factories in Atlanta of which Inman, Smith & Company was the largest and best known. Organized in 1896, Inman, Smith & Company started with thirty-five machines. By 1902, the company was operating 225 machines and employing 300 people in clothing manufacturing, when it was making 1,000 pairs of pants a day. In addition to the pants, overalls, and shirts made in the factory, it also sold shoes, notions, and furnishings. The men's clothing industry grew so fast that by the turn of the century the industry employed more women than did the cotton mills.[98] In just ten years the percentage of female industrial workers working in the men's clothing industry went from 5.7 percent to 32.2 percent.[99] Hugh had turned the company over the Edward while remaining involved from a distance. Others active in the company were John A. Smith, H. C. Leonard, and Hugh Richardson, Hugh's son-in-law.[100]

Along with the rise of cotton mills in Georgia, the manufacturing of woolen goods had also developed since the war. Hugh financially supported the Atlanta Woolen Mills, organized in 1896. It had a capital of $350,000 and did a business amounting to $500,000 a year. The plant also contained a cotton mill, and by 1902 this company employed 450 people. Its products consisted mainly of wool cashmere, Kentucky jeans, cotton warp, and hosiery yarns. W. M. Nixon was the president in 1902 and Hugh T. Inman acted as the vice president with J. D. Turner as the secretary. Edward, Hugh's son, served as one of the company's vice presidents.[101]

With their livelihoods depending so much on the cotton industry, the Inman family also began to encourage research into cotton as a crop. Samuel M. Inman was credited by the local newspaper as being instrumental in introducing new methods of cotton agriculture to the South. According to them, his interest in agricultural improvements led to a better staple of cotton and a larger yield per acre. They referred to him as the friend of cotton and classified him as a "cotton merchant and a capitalist."[102] When he retired in 1897, according to one historian "he had firmly established Atlanta as one of the preeminent cotton centers of the South."[103] However, the improvements in agricultural technology and methods were not sought strictly in the best interests of the farmers, but rather for the sake of cotton brokers such as Samuel M. Inman who desired a higher grade of cotton. This desire also led to further efforts in agricultural education, particularly in the production of cotton. The attention to agricultural education will be discussed further in chapter 3 of this study.

Another direct sideline of the production of cotton was the use of fertilizers. Cotton is a soil-depleting crop; after the first crop of cotton, the soil suffers significantly and yields decrease. With continued planting of cotton, the land stops producing. Hugh T. Inman took an interest in fertilizers, hoping to reverse much of the effect cotton growing can have on the land. Between 1879 and 1882 he had a license to sell guano with his office located at Board and Alabama streets.[104] Later he founded a guano company with Colonel George Washington Scott, the founder of Agnes Scott College. Scott had founded the George W. Scott Fertilizer Company, which merged with Comer Hull Company of Savannah to become the Southern Fertilizer Company. The Southern Fertilizer Company was later bought by Virginia-Carolina Chemical Company.[105] After the selling of his first fertilizer company, Scott joined Hugh in establishing the Kennesaw Guano Company, and in 1891 Inman was listed as a cotton and fertilizer merchant in the Atlanta city directory.[106]

Following Sam, John, and Hugh Inman was the second generation of the family involved in cotton trading and brokeraging. Edward H. Inman, Hugh's only son to live to adulthood, was a partner in the Atlanta office, along with his cousin, Frank M. Inman, Sam's youngest son. Edward joined the cotton business in 1903 and retired from the company in 1921.

Frank served on the New York Cotton Exchange for many years. Samuel M. Inman left the cotton business in 1896 after the death of his brother, John. With his retirement, the largest cotton business in the South, S. M. Inman & Company, was divided into three companies. One was Sanders, Swann & Company of Atlanta, which involved W. C. Sanders and James Swann, the former business partner of John H. Inman in Inman, Swann & Company. Sanders, Swann & Company became Inman, Akers, & Inman in 1903, then Inman, Howard & Inman in 1918, and in 1951 it became Inman, Howard & Company. Another was Inman & Company in Augusta. And lastly was Inman & Reed of Houston, which later became Inman, Nelms & Company. Sam continued to work with the Houston branch, having W. M. Reed, Hugh T. Inman, and Walker P. Inman as his partners. However, W. M. Reed may have been the only partner to be directly involved with the company, if any of the partners were.[107] Sam remained with Inman & Reed for five years,[108] retiring from active business in 1904.[109] Later Henry A. Inman, Sam's eldest son, formed Inman, Nelms & Company of Atlanta, and John Sanders formed Sanders & Company in Houston.[110] Each of these was a direct product of the earlier Inman firms. The cotton business proved to be as profitable for the second generation as it had been for the first.

An agency had to spend a substantial amount of money in the shipping of cotton, and to lessen this cost it would invest in the railroad company in its area. At least this way the broker could vote for discounts in cotton freight rates, or if the agency became the major stockholder in a railroad it could force similar changes. By owning stock in the local railroad, an agency could reap the benefits of free travel for itself or could recoup money it spent on shipping cotton. It was through the dry goods stores, the insurance companies, the cotton presses, and the railroads that cotton breathed new life into Atlanta. It was the Inmans' involvement in cotton and the wealth they accumulated that allowed them to expand into these other fields of business.

Railroads were the major means by which large quantities of cotton came into and out of Atlanta. Farmers shipped their cotton to Atlanta brokers by one of the seven rail systems, which in turn shipped it to cities on the coast or in the North. The cotton that went to port cities was then shipped to Northern and European cities by steamer.[111] Agencies often shipped cotton from New York or other ports to Liverpool if the market offered a better price there. John H. Inman's involvement with various railroads reflected the interest of cotton firms and their dependence on the railroad systems. This movement into the railroad industry from another business was not unusual because it was seen as being an extension of an interest in the shipping of goods, and none of the major leaders made the railroads their exclusive business.[112] In fact, none of them came into the railroads with the intent to build and patiently wait for profits to develop, but they came with the plan to "make transactional fortunes through the construction of new lines, speculation in and manipulation of securities, and investment in areas affected by the railroad."[113] This assessment of the role played by railroad investors and directors can be examined when one considers John H. Inman as an example. In the years following his initial success in Inman, Swann & Company, John, later regarded as one of the greatest railroad magnates in America, began investing in several railroads throughout the East.[114] Of John H. Inman's role Klein writes, "No man played a more important or less understood role in the [Great Richmond] Terminal than John Inman."[115]

The Richmond Terminal, incorporated in 1880 by Thomas Clyde and William P. Clyde, was a holding company for the Richmond and Danville Railroad, which began operating in 1856. Legally, the Richmond and Danville Railroad could not hold stock of the Richmond Terminal; therefore, the stock remained in private hands. The company's charter authorized it to subscribe to the capital stock of any railroad company chartered by North Carolina, South Carolina, Tennessee, Kentucky, Georgia, Alabama, or Mississippi with the only limitations being that only $5,000,000 of capital stock could be owned.[116] Two years later the Richmond Terminal applied for changes in its charter which allowed an indefinite increase in the amount of capital stock it could purchase, added Florida, Louisiana, Arkansas, and Texas, and included provisions for railroads it acquired and consolidated.

With the newer charter in place in 1882, the Richmond and Danville Railroad was able to expand rapidly and would nearly triple in size between 1886 and 1890. By 1883 the Richmond and Danville Railroad owned or controlled 847 miles of rail and the Richmond Terminal 1,657 for a total of 2,504, reaching from Virginia down the east coast and into central Alabama with branches serving the capitals of the states it passed through and most of the major cities of Virginia, the Carolinas, and Georgia.[117] "In 1885 the Richmond and Danville system consisted of 2,669 miles, of which 853 miles were directly owned and leased by the Richmond and Danville, and 1,816 miles were controlled by the Richmond and West Point Terminal Company," which is another name for the Richmond Terminal Company.[118] It acquired numerous smaller lines around the southeastern United States including the Asheville and Spartanburg, the Northeastern of Georgia, the Knoxville and Augusta Railway, and the Richmond and Mecklenburg Railroad.

This policy of rapid expansion created more problems for the Richmond and Danville and the Richmond Terminal because many of the acquired lines were run down and badly in need of repair. In order to afford the necessary expansion, the Richmond Terminal increased its capital stock three times in just nine months. In order for the Richmond and Danville to retain control over its holding company, it had to purchase half of the new stock, which was done by issuing more bonds and stock in its company. This process of raising money through an increase in stock to purchase the same from another company was a floating debt. Floating debts and floating loans are both money, which was borrowed, with no set amount due as monthly or yearly payments. The difference between the two was that a floating debt has no due date, except if demanded by the company loaning the money, and the floating loan, although having no installment payments, is all due at the end of a given period preset in the loan agreement.

In 1885, the Richmond Terminal agreed to sell $250,000 in Asheville & Spartanburg bonds to an allied firm, Inman, Swann & Company.[119] It is hard to determine what earlier connections Inman had with railroad companies, but the purchase of these bonds demonstrated John's interest in railroads and his use of his cotton company as a vehicle for accumulating power in the railroad industry. In 1888 the Railroad Commission's list of directors has John H. Inman listed as a director of the East Tennessee, Virginia and Georgia Railroad of the Central System and the Georgia Pacific Railroad and the Northeastern Division both of the Richmond and Danville System.[120] For many years he was also a major stockholder in the Central of Georgia Railroad, referred to as the "Central System" in the Georgia Railroad Commission reports.[121] By the late 1880s John's interest and investments in railroads were well established and are well documented.

Although the selling of the Asheville and Spartanburg bonds gave the Richmond Terminal temporary relief, the overall financial situation of the company was not pleasing. It was also about this time that the depression of 1884 caused problems for the company as well, and the decision was made to do away with the Richmond Terminal Company. Although the Richmond Terminal cost little to run, as a front it caused delays and complications in the Richmond and Danville's operations. The real reason for the establishment of the Richmond Terminal Company had been the charter, but it was no longer valid when the Virginia legislature authorized the Richmond and Danville to own capital stock in railroads, which did not connect to it.[122]

In order to dump the Richmond Terminal, a scheme was devised by William P. Clyde in which the Richmond and Danville would acquire the Richmond Terminal's major holdings, paying for them with capital stock it owned in the Richmond Terminal. The Richmond Terminal would accept payment in its own stock because the less stock available on the market, the more their other stock would be worth. The Richmond Terminal did not know what the Richmond and Danville was planning, not realizing that their own stock would be virtually worthless soon. After taking everything of importance from the Richmond Terminal except the Georgia Pacific Railroad, the Richmond and Danville dumped its remaining Richmond Terminal stock on the market at low prices.[123]

With the market flooded with cheap stock in the Richmond Terminal, it was easy for someone new to acquire control of the abandoned company. This new group of owners, talented financiers of New York assembled by General Thomas M. Logan, included Emanuel Lehman, Isaac L. Rice, George F. Stone, and Alfred E. Sully. Four days after the purchase the Richmond Terminal, the new owners put its preferred stock on the market, and in another month the company went from five to thirteen directors consisting of the original five plus John A. Rutherford, John G. Moore, Henry M. Flagler, Robert K. Dow, Simon Wormser, John Wanamaker, E. D. Christian, James B. Pace and John H. Inman.[124] In that same month the Richmond Terminal made its first payment and took possession of the Richmond and Danville Railroad. Once again, questions arose regarding the relationship between the two companies. Now the tail wagged the dog, for it was in a position, which was never intended for a holding company.

The Richmond Terminal Company began expanding with the East Tennessee, Virginia and Georgia Railroad, which had gotten into financial trouble when a depression hit while it was expanding. The owners of the line, Calvin S. Brice and General Samuel Thomas, were familiar with the Richmond Terminal Company, and they desired an alliance with the Richmond Terminal. This association was arranged through the ownership of East Tennessee stock by the Richmond Terminal. In order to raise funds to make the purchase, the Richmond Terminal issued six percent collateral trust bonds, which were taken by the First National Bank on the behalf of the syndicate including Calvin S. Brice, General Samuel Thomas, John H. Inman, George S. Scott, John G. Moore, Grant B. Schley, and John D. Rockefeller.[125] Another tie linking the Inmans with this rail was James Swann, Inman's business partner, who became a member of its executive board in 1887.[126]

After the take-over of the East Tennessee, Virginia and Georgia Railroad by the Richmond Terminal, another small railroad, the Central of Georgia, felt the pressures of outside interest trying to obtain control through its holding company. Although the stock was being purchased through New York, the identity of the buyer remained secret until the Richmond Terminal was revealed as the one backing this movement. The Georgia Company was organized under a North Carolina charter, intended as a holding company for the Central of Georgia Railroad and modeling itself after the Richmond Terminal. The charter allowed the company to buy, guarantee, or endorse securities of railroads in North Carolina or any adjoining state, and the company could operate and lease railroads but not build any. Founding members of the syndicate included Emanuel Lehman and four relatives that made up Lehman Brothers, John H. Inman and James Swann of Inman, Swann & Company, Edward W. Clark with the E. W. Clark and Company, Isaac L. Rice, John C. Calhoun, Patrick Calhoun and Alfred E. Sully.[127]

The Central of Georgia's president viewed the expansion of the East Tennessee, Virginia and Georgia Railroad as an aggressive act with the latter encroaching into the former's region. He responded with expansion plans of his own, which increased the railroad's debt by fifty percent.[128] Although the Central of Georgia did not belong to the Richmond Terminal the Terminal owned a significant amount of stocks and bonds in the Georgia Company, which led the Terminal to be concerned with the thought of expanding and increasing its debt. It appeared to be a no win situation for the Richmond Terminal, since the East Tennessee, Virginia and Georgia, was in competition with the Central of Georgia. The Richmond Terminal failed to unite these subordinates and instead was forced to turn over any profits to these companies that were demanding payments on money the Richmond and Danville had borrowed from them in order to make various purchases while rendering the Richmond and Danville Railroad unable to pay dividends to its stockholders.[129]

Throughout this turmoil among the various factions, John H. Inman remained elusive and noncommittal to any particular company or cause.

Since his involvement with the railroad industry began, he had participated in the purchase of the Richmond Terminal Company, the East Tennessee, Virginia and Georgia Railroad, and the Georgia Company. On each of these he had not only acted as a member of the executive committee of the Richmond and Danville but also as a private investor for himself and his firm. Also during the fall of 1887, after the establishment of the Georgia Company, Inman personally purchased 10,000 shares in the Central of Georgia Railroad, thereby covering the different fronts.[130]

Leaders and investors of the Central of Georgia Railroad wished for a president of the Richmond Terminal that would favor the Central of Georgia over the East Tennessee, Virginia and Georgia. Under pressure, Alfred E. Sully resigned as president and Emanuel Lehman resigned as a director of the Richmond Terminal. Someone was desired to settle the disputes between the warring factions. Nominated and supported somewhat by both factions, Inman was hesitant to take a position. But it was his diversification, which made him the most obvious choice for president of the problem-ridden company, since it was believed that his personal interest would lead him to desire a peaceful solution.[131] Not only were John H. Inman and his partner, James Swann, board members of the Georgia Company and owned the second largest piece of this company, but Samuel M. Inman and Hugh T. Inman were board members of the Central Railroad and Banking Company of Georgia, a division of the Central of Georgia, with all of the brothers owning some stock in that company as well.[132]

In 1888, John H. Inman was elected president of the Richmond Terminal Company.[133] According to John F. Stover, John H. Inman was the director of the Richmond Terminal Company from 1887–1890 and the director of the Richmond and Danville from 1889–1890. Previously, he had been a member of the board for an undetermined number of years.[134] But according to Klein, Inman did not take over the presidency of the Richmond Terminal Company until 1888.[135] One historian, noting that Inman hesitated to take the position, believed that taking on such a task meant he had an enigmatic and elusive personality.[136] His contemporaries, however, credited him with having such personal characteristics as "great financial abilities, vast personal magnetism, and boundless energy."[137] Although they might be biased, these quoted characteristics give a sense of Inman's strengths as perceived by his colleagues.

In the fall of 1888 a rumor was out that the Richmond Terminal Company was attempting to obtain control of the Central of Georgia by purchasing 120,000 shares of Georgia Company stock at $35 each. It was this purchase that some would later allege to be fraudulent, causing the downfall of the Richmond Terminal Company. Some contemporaries considered the acquisition of the Central of Georgia to be the "most important trade in railroads made in the South in twenty years."[138]

At a special meeting held in October 1888 from which John H. Inman and John C. Calhoun were notably absent, each sending letters explaining his absence and wishing it to be so noted, Emanuel Lehman proposed to sell the outstanding stock of the Georgia Company as well as $4,000,000 in bonds to the Richmond Terminal. Considering that the market price for stock in the Central of Georgia had ranged from $110 to $130 per share during 1887 and was currently running at $115, the proposal appeared to be a bargain.[139] However, there was a problem with the original bonds, which were the first lien on the company's stock, forcing a stock purchaser to guarantee interest on these bonds or buy them in addition to the stocks.[140] This additional cost went from making the acquisition of the Central of Georgia a bargain to making it an expensive procurement. The purchase, from which four directors and the president stood to gain personally, was approved by the board of the Richmond Terminal, which agreed to pay for all the Georgia Company stock and to buy $1,000,000 of the bonds, leaving the remaining $3,000,000 in bonds to be purchased soon afterward or to have the Richmond and Danville Railroad guarantee interest on them.[141] Holding shares in the Georgia Company and participating in the sale to the Richmond Terminal included Inman, Swann & Company with 15,592 shares, Emanuel Lehman with 24,379 shares, Inman, Swann & Company for E. P. Alexander with 4,154, and Isaac L. Rice with 7,634.[142]

Now that the decision had been made to acquire the Central of Georgia via the Georgia Company, the problem facing the Richmond Terminal was where to get the money, and a committee consisting of Inman, Thomas, and Scott was appointed to address the issue. Meeting the following month, the committee gave Inman a free hand to borrow the money by any means necessary and on any terms in order to expedite the deal. With this freedom, he formed a syndicate mainly within the Richmond Terminal Company, which was to advance the necessary money for the stock and $1,000,000 for the bonds. As Klein points out, John obviously exposed himself to charges of conflict of interest, not only in the stocks but also in the bonds as well since he had purchased $500,000 of bonds from his firm, Inman, Swann & Company, for the Terminal. But in December, the board ratified his acts and all of the transactions and the general company unanimously approved as well.[143] But the Richmond and Danville refused to pay interest on the bonds, which were not being purchased, giving no official reason and leaving the Terminal faced with having to purchase the bonds outright.

In the meantime, the Central of Georgia had run into its own financial problems due to an ambitious expansion called the Savannah and Western Railroad. Not only had the project used most of the company's liquid cash, but it had also given the company a sizable floating debt. In order to alleviate the problem, General Edward P. Alexander, president of the line, decided to issue $18,000,000 in bonds on the expansion line with the Central of Georgia guaranteeing interest on these. Inman and his associates took this opportunity to acquire the finances necessary to purchase the stocks of the Georgia Company by borrowing money from the Central of Georgia and using the new Savannah and Western bonds in a complex transfer to secure this loan.[144]

From the depleted Central of Georgia, Inman borrowed $3,000,000 through an intricate rearranging and shuffling of securities. Other factors, which had to take place in order for the acquisition to be accomplished, included the purchase by Hollins and Company, another firm holding stocks in the Georgia Company, of $5,000,000 worth of Savannah and Western stock at 95. The Richmond Terminal agreed to conclude the purchase from another syndicate consisting of John H. Inman, John C. Calhoun, Patrick Calhoun, James Swann, and Simon Wormser. Then the Central of Georgia Railroad loaned the Richmond Terminal $3,500,000 for the purchase of the Georgia Company's bonds. In addition Hollins and Company and E. W. Clark and Company, both stockholders of the Georgia Company, received $25,000 each in relation to claims arising from the negotiations, and the Central of Georgia paid the Georgia Company $25,000 to make up the difference between what the Richmond Terminal paid, 94, and the 95 demanded by Hollins and Company in the agreement.[145] After the bargaining ended, the Terminal emerged in possession of the Georgia Company's entire stock and all but $553,000 of its bonds.

However, the dealing was not yet complete because the Central of Georgia was short of cash and would not approve the loan agreed on previously unless the Richmond Terminal would cash the notes immediately.[146] To cash the notes immediately and to carry the Richmond Terminal's notes given for the purchase of the Georgia Company, Inman, Swann & Company formed another syndicate. In carrying the loan, Inman and Swann were able financially to benefit not only from the sale of the Georgia Company but also from the transaction itself. According to Stover the deal became more suspicious when the Central of Georgia voted John Inman and his associates a gratuity of $25,000 for helping to sell the bonds, which in turn permitted the company to lend $3,500,000 to the Richmond Terminal Company.[147] There is no mention of this by Klein.

The permanent financing was a problem, which was to be addressed by a committee consisting of Inman, Scott, and Thomas. For this dilemma Inman announced a new blanket mortgage for $24,300,000, which would provide the $5,000,000 needed for the Georgia Company transaction, and new mortgage was to be sold to a syndicate headed by

Inman, Swann, John C. Calhoun, Kessler and Company, and Maitland, Phelps and Company.[148] In the overall picture of the dealings of the Richmond Terminal Company, the numerous maneuverings of the syndicates may not appear to be important, but the sheer number of the syndicates alone demonstrate the complexity of the operations. They also show how many different angles of the business and the financial dealings in which John H. Inman played a role.

Questions of conflict of interest soon arose, and when the issue was pushed several years later, many would claim that Inman had intentionally misrepresented the condition, worth, and status of the Central of Georgia and that his syndicate had deliberately led the other lines into believing that the Central of Georgia posed more of a competitive threat than it actually did. From the evidence gathered for this study, it appears that John H. Inman intentionally misrepresented the value of the Central of Georgia Railroad and the status of the Georgia Company. He knew the value and status of the company since he was a major stockholder and a director, and he stood to profit from this business deal. The extent of his exact knowledge was never determined since the case never went to trial and no sources are available which tell his side of the story or even this side with conclusive evidence, demonstrating John's knowledge. Unfortunately, sources that might shed more light on this matter were not available through Norfolk Southern Railway, the successor of Southern Railway, which was the successor of the Richmond and Danville. The board minutes of the Richmond and Danville deal with the various mergers and by-outs, but they do not indicate whether Inman was ever tried in this case. All of this was speculative, but the fact that board members who stood to profit from the deal did not abstain from voting was factual and was against Virginia law.[149]

Regardless of the legalities, Inman had begun what was viewed by many as a very necessary step in the proper management of the Richmond Terminal. He confronted the task of integrating the many parts of the system both physically and financially. If the lines were consolidated, competition between the different systems would have been eliminated, and if all were managed by the Richmond Terminal, conflicting interest would also have been eliminated.[150] However, to accomplish such a feat, large amounts of money were needed for the purchase of the outstanding securities of each railroad. Realizing that this could not be achieved easily, Inman tried to force the three subordinates to cooperate.

Inman took over the presidency of the Richmond and Danville Railroad in 1890, serving in this capacity simultaneously as he served as the president of the Richmond Terminal. As president of the Richmond and Danville Railroad and the Richmond Terminal, John was in control of nearly 8,883 miles of railway[151] and twelve ocean steamers,[152] while the Louisville & Nashville Railroad, the second largest system in the southeastern United States, had only 2,400 miles.[153] In percentages, the Richmond and Danville system controlled over a quarter of the entire Southern rail mileage in 1890.[154] Businessmen with an interest in railroads occasionally referred to the collection of rails as the Inman System of Railroads, since John H. Inman was responsible for much of its expansion.

All of this came to a head when the *New York Herald* printed an exposé of the company's affairs. The article listed eight points of concern regarding the company and charged that many dividends paid periodically by Richmond Terminal subsidiaries had rarely been earned, and the Terminal's three systems had a floating debt, which had increased more than $13,750,000 in the preceding year. The article charged the Richmond and Danville Railroad had only earned 2 percent on its stock while paying 10 percent, therefore incurring a deficit of over $1,000,000. The company hid this shortage and the heavy losses of the auxiliary lines and transformed it into an imaginary profit by creative and deceptive bookkeeping. The Central of Georgia had not earned the 8 percent dividends it had paid, and the East Tennessee system could barely pay its own way, while most of its auxiliary lines were running on serious deficits.[155] To pay dividends, which some considered to be exorbitantly high, the company had sold off some of the securities that it had listed as assets.[156]

Immediately the Richmond and Danville prepared responses in hopes of recovering the confidence of the public and its stockholders. John did not deny the charges but claimed that once the company presented the reports to the public, everyone would see that the *Herald's* article was misleading and that the Richmond Terminal Company and its auxiliary lines were solvent. However, no one chose to address the main issues, which were the topics of the article, and the company's reputation suffered damage, making it very difficult to sell the company's bonds.

Also during this same time, the Central of Georgia was suffering from lack of funds. The selling of stock had put the company under a greater financial stress, and it had to be leased to the Georgia Pacific Railroad. The board of the Central of Georgia felt that the directors of the Richmond Terminal were ignoring them and that major decisions affecting the Central were being made without their input.

This discontent and ill feeling came to a head when Mrs. Rowena M. Clarke of Charleston, a minor stockholder in the Central of Georgia, sued the Richmond Terminal Company, claiming that the lease of the Central of Georgia to the Georgia Pacific was unconstitutional in Georgia. The state constitution of 1877 outlawed monopolies and stated that any contract between companies "which might defeat or lessen competition in their respective businesses" would be illegal.[157] Clarke won her suit, and the court appointed General Edward P. Alexander of New York, previously the president of the railroad, to act as temporary receiver of the Central of Georgia.[158] He originally gained the presidency in January 1887 succeeding William G. Raoul of Savannah as president, supported by John H. Inman and Samuel M. Inman. Under Alexander, the "Central of Georgia came completely under northern control."[159] The court also ordered that the Richmond Terminal could not vote on behalf of the 42,200 shares of the Central of Georgia stock it owned.[160] The Georgia Railroad Commission reported that the company was placed into receivership at the insistence of the minority stockholders in order to cancel its lease to the Georgia Pacific Railroad Company, which had previously been leased by the Richmond and Danville Railroad, and to "prevent the voting of the majority of the stock by the Richmond and Danville shareholders, who were alleged to have unlawfully bought the same."[161] The receivership became permanent when the Central of Georgia defaulted on its interest, and the courts appointed Hugh M. Comer of Savannah as receiver in July 1892. When the Central of Georgia went into receivership in 1892, it consisted of eight different lines: the main line, the Augusta and Savannah Railroad, the Southwestern Railroad, the Savannah, Griffin and North Alabama Railroad, the Upson County Railroad, the Chattanooga, Rome and Columbus Division, the Columbus and Rome Railroad, and the Buena Vista and Ellaville Railroad. Of these lines, six had been profitable, earning over $1,182,000 after expenses, while the other five had lost a total of $80,052.98.[162]

Rumors abounded that the Richmond Terminal Company, with its "reputation for extravagant expansion,"[163] was about to purchase the Baltimore and Ohio. But as president of the company, John H. Inman was sure that the future of his organization lay in the South.[164] In July of 1891, he announced that soon the general headquarters of the Richmond Terminal Company would be moved to Atlanta, which was closer to the center of the system. But financial difficulties plagued Inman's lines, and the expansion of the previous years proved to be detrimental to the Terminal. Small stockholders felt that they no longer had control over their companies since the Richmond Terminal Company had shown an interest and had purchased stock. The directors of the Richmond and Danville Railroad showed no loyalty to the lines and did not see them as serving a particular port or city, but rather as components of the larger system, often discounting the smaller communities and the lines that served them. These take-overs by the company were in line with the investments of the directors and were strictly for immediate profit rather than long-term gain.[165]

Although the board of directors insisted that positive reports regarding the railroads' financial status were true, soon John H. Inman admitted under pressure that there were several floating debts including one with the Richmond & Danville Railroad for $3,200,000, one with the Central of Georgia for $3,800,000, and one with the East Tennessee, Virginia and Georgia for $1,400,000. But even having acknowledged these large loans, John remained confident that the railroads would soon be able to pay them off. In November 1891 the board of the Richmond Terminal Company finally acknowledged in its annual report its inability to pay this immense debt. In hopes of saving the company, stockholders organized a special committee to explore reorganizing the company led by Frederic P. Olcott, president of the Central Trust Company.[166]

During the first few months of 1892, the Richmond Terminal Company remained in limbo waiting for the Olcott plan, deferring the election of directors and a president. Finally in March, elections were held and Inman retained his position as president, although he asked to be replaced as soon as possible.[167] With the increased instability and public unrest, John resigned as president of the Richmond Terminal Company soon afterward, and Walter G. Oakman, the operational executive of the First National group, replaced him.[168] The Richmond and Danville Railroad Company was reaching the peak of its mileage at this time. Oakman was to begin proceedings to cancel the contract by which the Richmond Terminal Company had purchased the Georgia Company. The board authorized him to bring suits in order to recover the money the Richmond Terminal Company overpaid for the securities of the Georgia Company. It alleged that the syndicate had only a short time previously purchased the securities at about half the price. The directors in question were to be called to account for their profits.[169]

In May 1892, Olcott's special committee was dropped and a new one was formed consisting of Samuel Thomas, a member of the 1883 syndicate that controlled the Richmond and Danville through stock,[170] W. E. Strong, and William P. Clyde, a former director who had dominated the management of the system in the early 1880s.[171] The new committee strongly suggested that J. P. Morgan of Drexel, Morgan and Company, seen as "wise in the art of rehabilitating embarrassed corporations,"[172] examine the Richmond Terminal property in the hopes that Morgan would agree to oversee the reorganization of the company.[173] Businessmen and politicians viewed the survival of the railroad as being very important to the welfare of the South.[174] After inspecting the company, Morgan found through an investigation by his representative, Samuel Spencer, who later served on the board of the Southern Railway with Samuel M. Inman,[175] that the company was hopelessly complex and the condition of its rails and rolling stock poor. On these grounds, Morgan refused to undertake the reorganization of the Richmond Terminal Company.

On 1 August 1892, the Richmond Terminal Company defaulted on some bond interest that was due.[176] On 23 August the courts put the company under the receivership of Walter G. Oakman, appointed by Judge Bond.[177] Oakman immediately prepared "a case against John H. Inman and his associates alleging fraud in the purchase by the Richmond Terminal Company of the securities of the Georgia Company."[178] The reply John H. Inman gave regarding the allegations was referred to as a masterpiece evading the charges but not denying that a swindle of gigantic proportions had been put over on the Richmond Terminal.[179] Unfortunately, details of the suit could not be located for this study.

In September 1892, stockholders held a special meeting and selected an almost entirely new group of men to serve as directors. William P. Clyde was the only one from the previous reign who returned with the new group.[180] Before this special meeting adjourned, a resolution passed requesting the newly elected directors to investigate the "past history of the company and its various transactions, and to employ such counsel and experts and take such steps as they may deem for the best interest of the company."[181] In December 1892, the company issued summons and complaints in the suit with the Georgia Company syndicate, and the case went before the New York Supreme Court.[182] There were the obvious conflicts of interest, and the charges claiming that most of the directors and board members of the Richmond and Danville were disinterested and ignorant of the Central of Georgia's affairs. The results of this case are unknown. It does not appear that any time was served if a conviction was ever handed down although a fine or the paying back of funds may have taken place, but there has been no documentation supporting this theory. However, it is known that John H. Inman had depleted much of his personal fortune by 1893.

Once again, the board members and stockholders asked J. P. Morgan and Company to take over managing the company, and it took much persuasion to convince Morgan to take on the failing Richmond Terminal system which Frederic P. Olcott and the Central Trust Company had been unable to save.[183] Olcott had developed a plan, which both physically and financially combined the three largest components of the system. The plan was not popular among the stockholders and therefore met its demise early. Drexel, Morgan and Company agreed to take over the reorganization in February 1893 and from the chaos emerged the Southern Railway Company.[184] The company still exists today as Norfolk Southern Railway.

Although John H. Inman had these obvious ties to the railroad industry, his interest went beyond the position of stockholder or director of a railroad. In 1891, he helped organize and then took over Tennessee Coal & Iron, an extension of his railroad interests.[185] Tennessee Coal and Iron was a successful business venture for Inman, which used convict labor.[186] Coal and iron were two important factors in the railroad industry, the coal being used for fuel and the iron for rails and the rolling stock. This was not his first contact with the coal and iron industry. The depression of 1884 and 1885 was the first opportunity Southern iron had to invade the Northern market, and this was the point when Southern iron began to receive attention of Northern investors. John H. Inman and John C. Calhoun led a delegation of wealthy investors through the South that included Andrew Carnegie, Frederic Taylor, and Abram S. Hewitt on a trip with the purpose "to spy out the land," as C. Vann Woodward referred to it.[187] After successfully scouting Southern ore regions, Inman bought extensive tracts of coal and iron land and invested heavily in secondary industries, among them the American Cotton Oil Company and American Pig Iron and Storage Company.[188] This involvement has led to some historians crediting John with having played an important role in developing the coal, iron, and steel industries of the South.[189]

During the 1880s, before his involvement with the Richmond and Danville Terminal Company, businessmen considered John to be one of the leading financiers in the United States due to the success of his cotton brokerage firm, Inman, Swann & Company. According to newspaper accounts, he commanded more capital in 1881 than all but two or three other men in New York, and personally his worth amounted to several million dollars by 1881.[190] By the age of 35, he was a millionaire several times over and "had ascended into the best of New York society."[191] Others found that the shrewd John H. Inman "was no man to let a literally golden opportunity slip past."[192] After resigning as president of the Richmond Terminal Company, Inman sought to regain his lost capital by the way he had gained much of it originally, through speculating in cotton. Unfortunately, the depression of 1893 hit soon after he began, causing Inman to lose even more money. The railroad scandal coupled with the lost of untold wealth lead to his early death. For three years he struggled to make a financial return. He died on 5 November 1896, in a sanitarium in New Canaan, Connecticut,[193] leaving his wife and six children with a mansion under construction on Fifth Avenue in New York City and only about half a million dollars. Although the reports make it sound as if he left his widow and small children destitute and although they probably had suffered a dramatic change in lifestyle, it should be noted that the youngest child would have been a young teenager and $500,000 was still a substantial amount of money. His estate was in such disarray at the time of his death that it took his brother, Sam, ten years to sort out the details of his debts.

Death in a sanitarium occurred again in 1910 when Hugh T. Inman died in a private one in New York where he was being treated for neurasthenia, which is a weakness of the nervous system, and in layman's terms is a nervous breakdown. He actually died of pneumonia but had suffered with neurasthenia for three months. Unlike John, it is uncertain that any event caused Hugh's collapse. It is possible that this was an inherited weakness. In any case, the Atlanta newspapers did not mention this, only that Hugh had been hospitalized while visiting New York. Family letters indicate that they did not tell anyone the reason why he had been hospitalized and that the family was concerned with his depression, refusal of food, and melancholy state.[194]

John was not the only Inman involved with or interested in railroads. Not only were Sam and Hugh directors of the Central of Georgia, but Hugh was also a director of the Northeastern Division Railroad, a subsidiary of the Richmond and Danville Railroad.[195] In 1891, when railroad magnate Jay Gould was looking for a location for his railroad facilities, including a new passenger depot, he considered the possibilities of Atlanta. On his trip to Atlanta, Gould was accompanied by his family and a large group of financiers and railroad men including John H. Inman. Immediately upon their arrival the Inman-Gould party, as the city council referred to it, received what the city council called "the courtesy of the city" and was ushered to the Chamber of Commerce for a meeting with leading businessmen of the city which included Mayor William A. Hemphill, Evan P. Howell, editor-in-chief of the *Atlanta Constitution*, Rufus B. Bullock, reconstruction governor of Georgia, Jack J. Spalding, an attorney, Captain James W. English, bank owner, Henry Jackson, Robert J. Lowry, future mayor and banker, L. J. Hill, former Mayor John T. Glenn, Julius L. Brown, Albert E. Thornton, and Hugh T. Inman. Mayor William A. Hemphill proposed this special treatment.[196] While Gould was in town investigating the possibilities, Hugh and his wife, Margaret Josephine Inman, and their daughters, Annie and Josephine, entertained Gould and his family with an elaborate party.[197] For such a warm, official reception, John H. Inman wrote a letter to the Atlanta City Council thanking them for how the party was "cordially received and royally entertained by your generous citizens," which was copied into the city council minutes.[198] Despite the efforts of the Inman family and the citizens of Atlanta, Gould decided not to start his business in Atlanta.

Samuel Inman played an important role locally with the railways, serving as a member of the Central of Georgia Railroad's board in 1883–1892.[199] It is unclear when Hugh left the board, but Sam resigned from the position just before Central of Georgia's elections late in 1891 due to the scandal with John and the Richmond and Danville system. He was instrumental in the establishment of the Southern Railway Company, and he served on its board of directors from 10 February 1896 until October 1912.[200] The company's connections with Sam were evident three years later when, out of respect, the Southern Railway Company's office closed and every engine and wheel stopped for a brief period of time during his funeral.[201] Under Sam's guidance, the Southern Railway organized the Atlanta & Birmingham Railroad, which was later purchased by the Atlanta, Birmingham & Atlantic Railroad.[202] While with the Southern Railway, he assisted the president, Samuel Spencer, who relied on Sam in matters concerning Georgia, particularly Atlanta.[203] Much of the Southern Railway's positive attitude toward Atlanta was due to Sam's close business relationship with Spencer and with the city.

Perhaps one of the most significant dealings Sam had with the Southern Railway System and the city of Atlanta came when the Southern was willing to place its new train yard in Atlanta if the city made certain concessions. Sam was in charge of selling the idea of a new train yard to the Fulton County Board of Commissioners. He was a logical candidate for this undertaking because everyone felt that he had interest in both Atlanta and the railroad and would not make any deal, which would not be beneficial to both. To convince the commissioners of his sincere regard for Atlanta, although he had been living in New York for eight years while settling John's estate, he commented that his "interest [was] with Atlanta. Where I have one dollar in the Southern Railway Company, I have fifty in Atlanta."[204]

His speech, printed in the *Atlanta Constitution*, pointed to the fact that with a new and larger terminal the city's ability to handle merchandise would increase and lower freight rates would benefit Atlanta economically.[205]   According to Inman, the local newspapers were depicting "the manufacturing industries . . . at a standstill on account of unjust discrimination in freight rates against Atlanta."[206] Although he found the city to be prospering more than ever before, he was sympathetic to its desire for lower freight rates and pointed out that no city in the country felt that it was getting fair freight rates. He considered himself to be an Atlantan with similar interests, stating, "I am an old freight man myself. I have shipped as much freight out of Atlanta as most of you here today, a great deal more than some."[207]

The Fulton County Board of Commissioners was persuaded by Inman's argument, feeling that the city would benefit greatly by agreeing with the concession required by the company. Under Sam's leadership, the Southern Railway system erected the Terminal Station in Atlanta, spending $2,250,000 and appropriately naming it Inman Yard. The new station consisted of a freight depot and what railroad enthusiasts considered to be one of the finest train sheds in the country.

At the time of his retirement as a director of the Southern Railway system in 1912, Samuel M. Inman was commended for his valued leadership of the railroad and for "his generous interest in the development of this community and of the South."[208] He was succeeded by John W. Grant, Hugh's son-in-law, who was regarded by the newspaper as a wise choice and in the best interest of the citizens of Atlanta. Grant was also from a railroad family, his father, William D. Grant, and his grandfather, John T. Grant, having built the Atlanta and West Point Railroad, and in 1888 the estate of John T. Grant held a position as a director of Atlanta's oldest railroad, the Western and Atlantic[209].

With the large amount of capital Sam acquired through the cotton trade and his interest in railroads, he was instrumental in bringing other industries to Atlanta. Joel Hurt, an Atlanta businessman who ventured in various fields including real estate, finance, insurance and civil engineering,[210] constructed the Equitable Building, which was Atlanta's first office building, and the Hurt Building. Hurt initiated the first streetcar line to run from his office buildings to the first planned suburb in Atlanta,

Inman Park, another Hurt venture, which was named after Hurt's friend and business associate, Samuel M. Inman. This venture came about as Atlanta's elites were moving from the edge of the business district to the new more fashionable suburbs along upper Peachtree Street and to Druid Hills.[211] Joel Hurt cut Edgewood Avenue for the streetcar;[212] construction of Atlanta's first electric railway was completed in August 1889 after Hurt built the first electric power plant in the city to provide electricity.[213] Chartered by an act of the legislature on 24 December 1886, the first streetcar line was the Atlanta and Edgewood Street Railway Company. Hurt's experience with railroad engineering led him to develop evenly laid track, which was well jointed and securely fastened. His cars were also different from the average streetcar of the day because they had a single motor in each car and used gear propulsion with controls at both ends. Hurt was able to finance this project with the support of members of the East Atlanta Land Company and others. One of Hurt's largest financial supporters and one of the incorporators was Walker P. Inman. Other supporters included C. W. Hubner, Asa G. Candler, H. E. W. Palmer, Peter Lynch, R. C. Mitchell, J. P. McDonald, J. G. Reynolds, A. F. Moreland, and P. H. Harralson.

The consolidation and development of the Street Railway Lines of Atlanta, another business venture of Joel Hurt, was also under the guidance of Sam and Walker Inman.[214] This movement created a single streetcar industry in Atlanta by combining Hurt's system with its competitors.

The original charter for the Atlanta and Edgewood Street Railway Company had permitted the laying of a line from the Five Points area downtown to the new suburb, Inman Park, via Edgewood Avenue. Eighteen months after the first electric trolley ran into Inman Park, Hurt was persuaded to consolidate the existing lines of horse cars with his electric ones. On 16 May 1891, Hurt was granted a new charter, which enabled him to form the Atlanta Consolidated Street Railway Company. Among the incorporates listed on the charter were several familiar names including Henry A. Inman, eldest son of Sam, Joel Hurt, and H. E. W.

Palmer.[215] The Atlanta Consolidated Street Railway Company brought together Atlanta's six streetcars, the Grant Park Electric Railway Company, the Fulton County Street Railroad Company, the Atlanta Street Railroad Company, the Metropolitan Railroad Company, the Gate City Street Railroad Company, and the West End & Atlanta Street Railroad Company.[216] On 4 April 1892, Hugh T. Inman petitioned the city council to allow Peachtree Street to be equipped with an electric car line. This petition coincided with Joel Hurt's plans to bring electricity to the same street.[217]

Hurt took the presidency of the Atlanta Consolidated Street Railway Company with Henry A. Inman, Henry Jackson, Robert J. Lowry, and H. E. W. Palmer as directors. These directors, along with Hurt, attended the American Street Railway Association Convention, a national convention that Hurt was instrumental in bringing to Atlanta.[218] The convention of 1894 brought together businessmen to share ideas on challenges facing their industry, and this was the first time it was held in the South. At this meeting and at others like it, Hurt was praised for his ingenious contributions, and he was elected the next president of the national organization.

Hurt held the presidency of the Atlanta Consolidated Street Railway Company six years, resigning in August 1897 to devote more time to yet another of his business interests, the Trust Company Bank of Georgia.[219] Hurt had received public criticism during the Cotton States and International Exposition of 1895, at which time he extended his streetcar lines to the exposition fair grounds at Piedmont Park and increased the cost of riding the streetcar from five cents to ten cents. Many people felt that he was taking advantage of the situation and was raising the cost simply for profit.[220] These were the reasons given for Hurt resigning from the streetcar business.

After Hurt's resignation, the *Atlanta Constitution* endorsed Samuel M. Inman as his successor as president of the Atlanta Consolidated Street Railway Company.[221] Although there is no record stating such, it appears that Inman turned down the opportunity to serve as the president. Instead Ernest Woodruff, Hurt's brother-in-law, was made acting president until a president could be elected, and Hurt retained his holdings and remained chairman of the board until one was elected.

In 1902, the Atlanta Railway and Power Company became the successor to the Atlanta Consolidated Street Railway Company with Ernest Woodruff serving as vice-president, and general manager and chairman of the board was Harry M. Atkinson, who purchased Hurt's holdings. The Atlanta Railway and Power Company was a merger of the Atlanta Consolidated Street Railway Company and the Atlanta Railway Company, its competitor. Atkinson and Hurt had fought each other bitterly, constantly applying for various concessions from the city council with each side having a set of lawyers and trying to become the city's only streetcar service provider. Samuel M. Inman and Thomas Jefferson Cooledge, a Boston banker, negotiated a settlement in which Atkinson purchased Hurt's interest in the Atlanta Consolidated Street Railway Company, thereby completing Hurt's removal from the streetcar business.[222]

Soon afterward the Atlanta Railway and Power Company merged with the Atlanta Rapid Transit Company forming the Georgia Railway and Electric Company, predecessor of the present Georgia Power Company, with Atkinson retaining the position of chairman of the board. Walker P. Inman was one of the original directors of the Georgia Railway and Electric Company. Other directors of interest included C. R. Spence, Thomas Jefferson Cooledge, Robert F. Maddox, Eugene P. Black, and Albert E. Thornton, all leading businessmen of Atlanta.

The Atlanta Inmans were not alone in their support of various streetcar companies. In New York City, John played a role in the New York Rapid Transit Commission from its inception, although documentation relating to this matter states little more than that he was involved and does not indicate at what level.

Just as factors had done, brokers were now buying, storing, shipping and selling cotton on a large scale while taking care of the various details involved. They could not risk fires and floods destroying their investments, causing a loss of capital, and it was from this necessity that insurance companies in the new South were born. Many of the insurance companies in Atlanta had cotton brokers on their boards or acting as directors or presidents, showing the strong connection between cotton and those trading it and those needing a means of insuring it. Once again, necessity was the mother of invention, only in this case cotton was the mother of invention. Cotton may have been the driving force behind much of Atlanta's desire for insurance, but it was not the only business to benefit from it. Real estate, particularly buildings, was prone to destruction by fires, and many of Atlanta's most traumatic events centered on fires. The Inman family, with interests in insurance for both their cotton and their real estate, was instrumental in bringing numerous insurance agencies to Atlanta; however, most of the insurance companies were from New York and other Northern cities and simply had regional headquarters in Atlanta after the Civil War.[223]

For many years, Samuel M. Inman was a director of the Equitable Life Insurance Company of New York and of the Equitable Life Assurance Society of Georgia. He was one of the first directors of Atlanta Home Insurance Company, a Joel Hurt business venture organized in September 1882 with the purpose of not only providing insurance but also keeping capital in Atlanta, serving for an undetermined length of time.[224] Hugh and Sam each owned $10,000 worth of shares in the Atlanta Home Insurance Company, which made them two of the largest stockholders in that company.[225] Joel Hurt also owned $10,000 of stock in the Atlanta Home Insurance Company. Perhaps most surprising of the subscribers was James Swann of Inman, Swann & Company, New York.[226] Another large stockholder in the company was Walker P. Inman, with $3,000 worth of shares.

Not only was Sam a stockholder and a director of the company, but he was also a member of the four-man committee appointed to examine the subscriptions and to report on them when enough money had been raised. Samuel M. Inman served on the subscription committee with Thomas G. Healey, builder of the Healey Building, J. H. Mecaslin, secretary and treasurer of the Board of Aldermen, and Jacob Elsas, city council member. With this extensive growth in the insurance industry, Atlanta soon became the leading Southern city in the business, behind only New York and Chicago in the country.[227] The family interest remained in insurance during the next generation as well with John W. Grant acting as a director of the Southern Mutual Insurance Company.[228]

Like his relatives in Atlanta, John moved into the insurance field as the demand for its services increased. He served as a director of five companies: American Surety, Home and Liberty Insurance, Home Insurance, Liberty Insurance; and the Royal Insurance Company in England.[229] There are few details about his level of involvement with these companies. He was probably a large financial supporter of at least one of them. Of course with his interests in cotton, which had to be shipped either by rail or by steamer, and his interest in railroads, insurance would have been very important to him as well.

As itinerant merchants in the earlier years, the Inmans offered dry goods to farmers for the promise of their cotton crop after harvest. Often these crops were in the fields, and in some instances they had not been planted yet. The extension of credit was a critical part of their role, and it enabled the farmers to survive from year to year in hopes of one year producing an especially large cotton crop to break the cycle. There was a large risk involved with offering credit to farmers, and most learned that they did not want to risk their entire business on an annual cotton harvest that could be the victim of the weather and insects. Others wanted more control over the credit they offered farmers and the interest they charged, putting themselves at less risk.

It was this shift in thinking that led cotton brokers to establish a number of banks and financial institutions in the South. These credit-extending institutions, which were ideally to help the average farmer, speculated in cotton as well.[230] These banks had the financial capability to speculate; and with most of them having cotton brokers and agents on the boards and acting as presidents, they also had the inside knowledge to make it profitable. These banks extended credit to farmers on their cotton crop with their farmland being collateral. If the crop covered the credit, then the farmer was in the clear for another year, paying the bank interest. If the crop fell short of the amount of the extended credit, creditors pursued foreclosure on the farm and the land became the property of the bank. In turn the banks became the owners of vast amounts of land throughout the countryside, which became available through various means.

The collateral was not always the farm, and the debtor was not always a farmer. Now that there were more banks with the capability of extending credit and not only to people with cotton crops, more people in urban areas were getting loans, and they too were losing their property or were forced to sell in order to pay back their debts. With hopes of making fortunes like others were doing, many borrowed money to start businesses, invest in industry, or purchase real estate. Many realized too late that if they were to compete with the elite businessmen of the city, more was needed than startup capital.

Just after the war cotton brokers often provided such services as extended credit and financial advice for their customers, including investments and general accounting. Things progressed to the point that these brokers came to found banks or participate in some capacity in the banking institutions of their communities, and the Inmans took this natural step. Before the Civil War, Walker and William Inman both were employed in banks in Atlanta, and in 1861 William attended a convention of bankers known as the "Bank Convention of the Confederate States," a meeting held in Atlanta for the purpose of providing financial aid to the new government.[231] Another important player in the Inmans' business, Alfred Austell, also attended the convention. Immediately following the end of the war, the need for a bank in Atlanta was evident. On 2 September 1865, a group of concerned businessmen from Atlanta, among them Austell and Walker P. Inman, met in New York City to found Atlanta National Bank, the first of many such banking ventures to be launched in the emerging city.[232]

In the 1880s, Sam was a director and Hugh was the president of the Atlanta National Bank, the same one Walker had helped to found years earlier. Hugh remained a director and vice president of that bank for many years,[233] and he was also an original director of Traders Bank of Atlanta, chartered on 24 October 1887, which in 1890 became the American Trust and Banking Company.[234] By 1890, the banking industry in Atlanta included eighteen private or joint stock banking institutions with a combined capital exceeding $2.5 million and with net deposits totaling $60 million. Sam was also a director and stockholder of the Lowry National Bank and of the Trust Company Bank of Georgia, a business venture of Joel Hurt's.[235] Samuel M. Inman became a director of Trust Company of Georgia by purchasing $5,000 worth of stock in the company at its infancy. Walker was the original president of the old Fourth National Bank, which began operation in 1889 as a state bank under the name the American Trust and Banking Company, and he served as the vice president of the Fourth National Bank in 1902. Walker P. Inman's son-in-law, James R. Gray, was the vice-president of the American Trust and Savings Bank after it converted into a national bank in 1896 and he served the Fourth National Bank as a vice-president.[236]

John's greatest involvement in financial institutions was with the Fourth National Bank of New York, and although there are indications that he was involved with other banks in New York, none of them were identified in researching for this study. The extent of his involvement with the banks remains unclear, yet it appears that he chose banks, which might help, in his financial dealings with the Richmond Terminal Company.

As always, following in their fathers' footsteps was the second generation of Inmans. In 1912, Frank M. Inman became a director of the Lowry National Bank, which became the Atlanta & Lowry National Bank and later the First National Bank, a position he held until 1933.[237] Edward H. Inman was a director of Trust Company of Georgia Bank, the First National Bank, and the Atlanta & Lowry National Bank.[238] John W. Grant, Hugh's son-in-law, served as a director of several Atlanta banks including Atlanta & Lowry National Bank,[239] and as a vice president of Citizens and Southern National Bank.[240]

The Inmans' involvement with these financial institutions enabled them to encourage industries that they felt were beneficial to the city through loans. It also enabled them to protect their own financial investments by extending loans to cotton farmers and local businessmen, which made the possibility of the acquisition of real estate rather easy through foreclosures. Real estate was a sound investment in a growing city like Atlanta, and best of all it was not subject to the potential crashes as the cotton market.

As Atlanta grew, so did the market for real estate, and like other businessmen of their time, the Inmans bought land and buildings as investments, and they found themselves acquiring land in credit foreclosures via their involvement with local banks.[241] In a rapidly growing city like Atlanta, purchasing cheap land and improving that land was a moneymaking occupation. Sam's real estate holdings were numerous and valuable, most of them around the Terminal Station. At the cost of $75,000, he built the five story Terminal Hotel on the corner of West Mitchell Street and Madison Avenue, with 75 bedrooms, 18 private baths, and a parlor on each floor.[242] The hotel was close to the station in order to encourage weary travelers to stay there. Sam also owned part of the Terminal District, the area bordered by Madison Avenue, Mitchell Street, Forsyth Street, and Nelson Street. Fire destroyed this property, including the Terminal Hotel, on 8 May 1908, with property loss alone totaling $400,000, which left Sam the heaviest loser of all the property owners involved. Walker P. Inman's estate suffered a $35,000 loss.[243] Insurance covered 80 percent of Sam's losses, and he was able to rebuild the district immediately. The Terminal Hotel was rebuilt and suffered the same fate thirty years later in what was the deadliest fire in the history of the city at that time. The five-story structure was set afire by an explosion in the basement; thirty-four people died.[244]

The family tradition in real estate and land ownership continued extensively in the second generation, whose members not only inherited extensive tracts of land but also invested in real estate of their own. Frank M. Inman, like his father, had acquired a large amount of land near the Atlanta Terminal Station before Sam's death. Possibly he had received an early inheritance, but he also could have invested in the heart of the city on his own.

Sam's other real estate interests included the East Atlanta Land Company, which developed Inman Park.[245] The other large stockholders included Joel Hurt, the planner behind this venture, Asa G. Candler, and Walker P. Inman; the purpose of this syndicate, formed in 1886, was to integrate streetcars and suburban development.[246] The creation of Inman Park did much for the development of the city by allowing residents to work downtown and live in a quiet neighborhood of large houses easily accessible via Edgewood Avenue, which was laid out by Hurt. The neighborhood, an immediate success, was the home of many wealthy Atlantans including Asa Griggs Candler, founder of Coca-Cola, Benjamin Harvey Hill, lawyer and politician, and former governors Allen D. Candler, of Georgia, and Alfred H. Colquitt.

After leaving Inman, Swann & Company, Hugh moved to Atlanta and began investing in real estate, beginning by purchasing land on which to build a home at the present site of the Atlanta Apparel Mart at the corner of Peachtree and Harris streets. His early ventures and investments after his return to Atlanta were successful, and in 1879 his personal property in Fulton County had a value of $41,460, much of this being in real estate. His interest in real estate continued to be important to him throughout his life.

Hugh's property included the famous Kimball House, "the most imposing structure in the city,"[247] which he gave to his son-in-law, John W. Grant, as a wedding present in 1893, a gift called the "largest and most historic gift ever given in Atlanta."[248] John W. Grant married Annie Martin Inman on 11 April 1893. He was the only son of William Daniel Grant and Sarah Frances "Sallie Fannie" Reid. William Daniel Grant had made his fortune in railroad construction with his father, John T. Grant. He lost his wealth in the war and rebuilt it with convict labor during Reconstruction as a member of Grant, Alexander & Company and then with the Penitentiary Company Three. John W. Grant's sister was Sarah Frances Grant Jackson Slaton, the wife of Governor John Marshall Slaton.

Hugh had helped finance the second building of the Kimball House after the first one burned in 1883. In the scheme of bigger, better and new, the second Kimball House was one story taller and 117 rooms larger.[249] The first Kimball House had opened in 1870 with six stories, making it the largest hotel in the South, and it was the first building in Atlanta to have a central heating plant and safety passenger elevators. Due to some financial problems, Hannibal I. Kimball was forced to use the land on which he was building the new hotel, the site of the first one, to finance the second one. A group of prominent businessmen in Atlanta, who accepted the land as collateral, were financially responsible for allowing H. I. Kimball to rebuild his hotel, which was seven stories tall and completed in 1885.[250] Over a period of time, Hugh T. Inman bought everyone else's share in the loan and became the sole owner of the land. Kimball was not in the financial situation that he had been in the first time he built the hotel; and when he could not make payments on his loans, Hugh became the owner of the Kimball House, assuming the debts totaling $280,000.[251] The Kimball House was a very important structure in Atlanta for over half a century and remained property of the Grant family until it was demolished in 1959.[252]

Another real estate interest of Hugh's was Ansley Park, an early residential community developed by E. P. Ansley at the cost of over $1 million.[253] As part of his fee in fostering the development of Ansley Park, Hugh received between six and ten acres of land. A tract of this land was later owned by Edward H. Inman, Hugh's son, who built a house at 205 The Prado, which suffered from two attic fires, prompting Edward to build what was jokingly referred to as a concrete house among family members, the Swan House, now one of the historic houses owned by the Atlanta Historical Society. Today part of the original tract of land in Ansley Park is Westchester Square, and a street, Inman Circle, remembers the Inman family there.[254] Real estate was only an investment with

Hugh, not a business; most of his investments in real estate were in property north of the city.[255]

Beyond these examples of the Inmans' real estate ventures and holdings, there were many other buildings and pieces of property owned by the family. The Atlanta City Council Minutes are peppered with decisions allowing the Inmans to build new and to destroy existing structures. Also listed are numerous petitions for special requests such as connecting into the city's sewer that did not run along the street to the front of the property, cutting a city street through one's property to improve access, or destroying a sidewalk in order to install underground industrial boilers. All of these petitions stood to enhance the real estate, increasing its value. The street addresses on many of these pieces of property covered much of downtown Atlanta around the turn of the century and included South Broad, W. Mitchell, Madison, Forsyth, Peters, Hunter, Alabama, S. Pryor, Whitehall and Wall streets.[256]

Although they came close, not all of the Inman's business dealings fit into these previously discussed categories. Other business involvements of Hugh's included Moore, Marsh & Company, a wholesale dry goods business, and Atlantic Ice & Coal. The degree of his involvement is undetermined in each of these. It is likely that he was a financial backer but was not involved in the daily running of these businesses. He also attended the opening of different types of businesses including the Atlanta Milling Company, a mill for grinding flour, but whether he had a financial interest in the company is unknown. The second generation also had undertakings, which were diversified as well. Frank was the treasurer of the Blount Carriage and Buggy Company of Atlanta.[257] Edward's business ventures included a directorship of the Atlantic Ice & Coal Company, a company purchased by his father just before his death, which he had no desire in running,[258] and investments in MacDougald Construction Company, his brother-in-laws' company.[259] In the next generation, Hugh T. Inman, II served as vice president and secretary of MacDougald Construction Company. Because of his interest in autos, Edward joined Frank Steinhauer and Captain Joe Brown Connally and formed the first local automobile agency in Atlanta, representing the Cadillac Company. Edward was also the president of the Kimball House Company, which was the property of his brother-in-law, John W. Grant.[260]

Cotton may not have returned to the prominent position of "king" following the Civil War, but for the Inmans and others in the cotton business it remained a despot of remarkable power. It was cotton that had supported the Inmans' plantation in eastern Tennessee, and cotton, which had been the reason for the bartering trade along the rivers. Although family legend is that few surviving bales of cotton at the end of the war had established the family in three cities in four different businesses, the family might also have had money reserved in a New York or English bank under William's direction. Whatever the source of their startup capital, the success of cotton, returning as a cash crop, enabled the family to grow from itinerant merchants into cotton brokers. It was cotton that created the family's wealth and spurred new business interests for the family, including insurance, banking, railroads, fertilizer, and real estate. Although local newspapers referred to Samuel M. Inman as an Atlanta pioneer and financier, it is easy to see how that term applied to the entire Inman family.[261] However, the success of their various ventures is due to their access to Northern capital with a link provided by John and William. John H. Inman claimed to have directed over $100,000,000 in Northern capital to the South.[262] It was the investment of such capital that spurred the growth in industry, which the Southern region of the United States so desperately needed.

Although the Inmans were active with various enterprises, which were directly and indirectly connected with the cotton business, their interest extended to many other areas. Their vast holdings in several major businesses were just the tip of the iceberg. In one form or another, the Inmans were involved in numerous businesses, touching many different parts of Atlanta industry. However, according to Don Doyle, this diversification in investments was not unusual among men of wealth who linked their fortunes to their community,[263] and the names of many of the businessmen the Inmans were in these ventures with appear again and again along with the Inmans in many of the same ventures. These entrepreneurs cooperated in establishing and bringing many different businesses to Atlanta.[264] Therefore, the Inmans were not unique in their philosophy in business, but having the funds that enabled them to enjoy this extensive diversification may be what made them different from most. Alliances among the elites were not limited to cooperation in business but included the intermarrying of the children of upper class, closing the groups and solidifying their positions.[265] With the children and their grandchildren of these marriages began the practice of depending more upon birth rather than own personal achievements to justify their position in society.[266] This group of families, referred to as a constellation by Doyle, retained their positions through their association with each other.[267]

Diversification not only protected one's financial holdings but also put one in a position to meet others in the community with similar financial and social standings, making alliances to establish other businesses in other dealings. To back a business venture with significant funds made one a director, but Doyle also sees being a member of the board of directors as proof of a certain social status.[268] However, wealth and business position alone did not gain one entry into elite society, and chapter 3 will discuss in greater detail the clubs and organizations, which helped particular families to maintain their elite status.

Much of the advantage that the first generation had over previous generations following the Civil War was their ability to do business on a national and international level. Before the Civil War only the South's cotton was a large national and international product. But after the war advancements in transportation and shipping such as the standardization of the railroad gauge and the increased availability of dependable communication enabled businessmen of the New South to operate on a much larger scale, to diversify in their investments, and to open up opportunities that before did not exist. That old crop, cotton, remained the main investment and the driving force of the New South, but it was also a way to other ends, allowing diversification and industrialization. King cotton had found a more far-reaching purpose.

2

BOOSTERISM:
The Inmans in Civic Life

Southern businessmen had long been involved in the activities of local government, since decisions made on that level had great bearing on their prospects for financial success. Moreover, the taking up of civic duties was an important form of city boosterism, and according to Don Doyle "most business and civic leaders in the 19th century saw the job of city building as their responsibility."[269] Boosterism was the idea that "a few earnest citizens could boom any town into a bustling metropolis."[270] And "dedicated to the tireless promotion of their city's growth and improvement,"[271] those businessmen who promoted the city formed a civic group all to themselves, bound together by their similar desires.[272] The participation of Southern businessmen in local politics was not new, but what was new was that these politicians actively pursued Northern capital for Southern industry. A businessman was considered successful if his business prospered, and his business grew according to his city's growth. The development of a city and of its population was a sign of an expanding economy, and such growth was encouraged in a variety of different ways. The businessmen who strove to achieve such growth and expansion subscribed to Henry W. Grady's New South mentality. They wanted their businesses to be successful and for Atlanta to develop economically, and they saw Northern capital as a necessary means of accomplishing these goals. These businessmen felt they knew what would aid the city in growth. Boosters not only sought for fair freight rates and advantages for industry but also wanted to enlarge the population by encouraging people to come live in their cities. The promise of a better way of living encompassed good paying jobs, public schools, churches and other civic institutions, and even clean drinking water. This cooperation between the municipal government and the private entrepreneurs for the improvement and enhancement of the city is the form of boosterism James Michael Russell refers to as the "American System."[273]

However, everyone did not desire growth; instead many wished their towns to remain small and to retain the social structure and order, which had existed prior to the Civil War. They felt that economic expansion would result in a disturbance of the communities' traditions and, contrary to the beliefs of the boosters, would not result in a better quality of life. While anti-industrialization and anti-growth were characteristics of older towns like Mobile and Charleston, Atlanta was a young city wishing for rapid expansion and not facing entrenched conservative interests that opposed modernization. The growth of industry did not disturb Atlanta because it did not have an established economic order; however, that does not mean that all the citizens of Atlanta were convinced that new businesses and the changes they brought would be beneficial to the city. But there were businessmen and politicians in power who, feeling that development was necessary, became boosters of the New South and nudged the region away from an agrarian toward an industrial economy.

Many of the policies adopted by business leaders and public officials were intended to distance Atlanta from the surrounding region, urging the city to accept Northern investment and not to cling to the ethos of the Old South.[274] Although advocates of a New South embraced many goals that conflicted with antebellum ideals, they also paid homage to the Old South and treated the Confederate veterans with utmost reverence.[275] Many of the political leaders following Reconstruction subscribed to this recipe for success. They glorified the war and the plantation way of life, yet they spoke of industry and the need for outside capital, which earlier they had viewed as evil Yankee notions. Early in the Reconstruction era, Atlanta's business leaders had decided to join with the North and demonstrated their willingness to pursue progress,[276] promoting it as a necessity for survival.

Most boosters were businessmen who stood to gain financially if the city succeeded. There were several different ways in which a booster could actively encourage the growth of the city. Many businessmen joined the Chamber of Commerce, a voluntary group that favored economic development and diversification. Among other things, it energetically pursued fair freight rates from the various railroads that ran through Atlanta. One such case was brought before the Railroad Commission of Georgia when the Atlanta Chamber of Commerce sued the Southern Railway and Steamship Association in 1886. In their petition to the commission, the chamber of commerce accused the railroad of driving up their earnings through contracts, a policy known as pooling, which was in violation of article 4, section 2, paragraph 4 of the Constitution of the state of Georgia. These pooling contracts, according to the Atlanta Chamber of Commerce, allowed merchants of Nashville, Tennessee, to rebill, or double charge, which was "an unjust discrimination against every city in Georgia."[277] Of course, every city in Georgia was not the concern of the Atlanta Chamber of Commerce, which called for the commission to "enforce the laws of the land and protect the rights of the people."[278] The chamber of commerce also blamed the contracts with creating monopolies and violating the state constitution in respect to competition. The commission agreed with the chamber and notified the railroads of this ruling.[279]

Although businessmen in Atlanta had a habit of complaining that the freight rates were unfair to them, an investigation of the rates in 1890 by the Interstate Commerce Commission found that there was at least one railroad, the Western and Atlantic, which favored Atlanta and Chattanooga with lower rates than any of the stops between these two cities.[280]

The Chamber of Commerce also gave businessmen a forum in which they could come together and discuss issues of mutual interest. Perhaps one of the most important functions of the Chamber in the early days was the posting of the prices of commodities, something that was particularly important to the cotton business. One such example of the Chamber's interest in the cotton market and its general effect on the local economy took place in the depression of 1893. Since money had become scarce, the operation of the cotton market was difficult, and without the movement of that all-important cash crop, Atlanta's economy would greatly suffer. The president of the Chamber of Commerce, Stewart Woodson, looked into ways to eliminate this problem. Walker P. Inman was a member of a committee, along with J. C. Oglesby, E. P. Chamberlin, M. C. Kiser, and Joel Hurt, which on the behalf of the Atlanta Chamber of Commerce was to persuade banks to issue clearing-house certificates, based on their resources and credit, to serve as currency during the crunch. The banks, looking into the committee's assessment of the situation, agreed promptly to begin to issue certificates that relieved the problem and enabled the cotton crop be sold at market.[281]

Other similar organizations, which sprang up, in Atlanta before the turn of the century included the Atlanta Mechanics' Institute, the Atlanta Agricultural and Industrial Association, and the Atlanta Manufacturers' Association, all which were founded in 1872. The German Manufacturing Association followed in 1875. Other associations in Atlanta included the Young Men's Business League, also called the Business Men's Association, of which Samuel M. Inman served as chairman 1906–1907 and the Atlanta Manufacturers' Association, which he served as president of in 1888.[282] Surviving through the turn of the century, the Atlanta Manufacturers' Association, the strongest of these organizations, was designed to "familiarize capitalists with facilities in the city,"[283] and it succeeded in bringing a cotton factory, among other things, to Atlanta. In 1873 it was also successful in persuading the city council to remove all taxes, except real estate taxes, on all existing and future cotton, wool, and iron factories in the city. Although there was this exception, the decision obviously had a profound effect on the success of these factories and attracted new ones as well.[284] The end result of the encouraging of industry was clear; to boost industry was to boost the city into more rapid growth and expansion. Boosters also achieved their goals by seeking and winning elected offices, serving on the county commission, the city council and its committees, the board of aldermen, and at times in the office of mayor. Promotion of the city's growth was the primary function and role of the municipal government, according to Atlanta's businessmen.[285]

It was because they wished to promote Atlanta that the Inman family became involved in the city-building enterprise by holding a variety of political and civic positions. Their influence did not always hinge on whether a member of the family had a position in the local government, but also whether a friend or business partner held an elected position of power. Although some members of the Inman family did not aspire to public stations, all the men in the family, according to a former governor, "exerted a powerful influence upon their epoch and environment."[286] There were various levels of local government in which businessmen and industrialists could participate, and the Inman family at one point or another had members involved or holding positions in nearly every position of service available.

In 1874, Atlanta adopted a new municipal charter, making it easier for the elected boosters to achieve their goals and enabling business leaders to assume control of municipal affairs in Atlanta. The charter reconstructed the city government and placed drastic limitations on expenditures and debts. Forty-nine business leaders, sixteen of whom were among Atlanta's wealthiest citizens, were appointed by the city council of 1873 to write this new charter, which created the Board of Aldermen, a financial watchdog approving all the council's expenditures. The main objective of the new charter was to "reduce municipal spending and depoliticize city government."[287]

Although it was the Board of Aldermen that served as controller of the purse strings, it was up to the council to make proposals. The Board of Aldermen, dominated by businessmen, halted much of what today would be seen as social spending.[288] These cutbacks to the city's less prosperous citizens translated into the lack of proper sewer systems, paved streets and street lights in residential neighborhoods, and also included cuts in money for public schools, health care and poor relief.[289] With the business leaders as aldermen, the actions of the board reflect the priorities of the business leaders, focusing attention and tax money on the business districts, justified in the hope of attracting other businesses to the city. In Atlanta during Reconstruction and the Victorian period there was not a working-class political force. There had been attempts by members of the working class to take positions in the city's government, but they were unable to be elected. Often their employers threatened them into submission. Although the African-American population also felt the pinch of the elitist government, their personal dislike and fear of the working-class Caucasians, and vice versa, prevented a joining of forces and left them siding with the business elite and often refusing to support African-American candidates.

If the local newspapers accurately displayed Samuel M. Inman's popularity, he could have had any position in local or state government, but he chose to remain out of the sphere of politics as an elected official. In October 1882, the *Atlanta Constitution* nominated Sam Inman for the office of mayor in an attempt to convince him to run in the 1883 election. The paper interviewed a number of Atlantans regarding this proposal, and almost all interviewed were overwhelmingly supportive of him. Those interviewed made glowing comments like Captain John Keely, who was quoted as saying, "I think Sam Inman would make an excellent mayor" and W. C. Dodson was reported to have said, "I will vote for Inman for anything."[290] The journalist who authored this supportive article of Samuel M. Inman is not identified, but with Inman's close relationship to Henry W. Grady, Evan P. Howell, and others who worked for the paper, it could have been almost anyone. This was the overwhelming verdict of the eighty-nine people interviewed; however, there were a few who refused comment regarding their support for

Inman, although the writer of the article noted, "such a unanimous and enthusiastic approval as is seldom given to any man."[291] The following day the paper ran a card from Sam Inman to the editors of the *Atlanta Constitution* declining to let his name be entered into the race for mayor.[292] The note began, "Entirely without my knowledge, within the past few days my generous friends have presented my name for the mayoralty of Atlanta in a manner which is almost irresistible with me, and which places me under a life-long debt of gratitude to them."[293] In declining, Sam feared that others would think he was indifferent to the welfare of Atlanta, but he pointed out that as a private citizen he has been forwarding the interest of the city through various means. To his friends, who put his name forth in the mayoral campaign, Sam wrote, it "strengthens my gratitude towards our big-hearted city, and impels me to renew my pledges to study and work for the good of Atlanta with all the means in my power as a private citizen."[294] On the same page of the paper the editors of the *Atlanta Constitution* note that this was "the most general and flattering invitation ever extended any citizen of Atlanta."[295] They noted that they did not print the responses of everyone interviewed, but that their selection of interviews to be printed was not biased in any way. This type of flattery was typical for its day and perhaps occurred to other business leaders the newspaper desired to see serve in political positions. If nothing else, this glowing recommendation demonstrates how elites were desired and courted for political offices, perhaps simply by their friends and status equals.

Governor Alexander Hamilton Stephens, who had just been elected the previous fall, died 4 March 1883. A week later, the *Daily Post Appeal* wrote that Sam Inman was its first choice for governor.[296] On the following day, the *Daily Post Appeal* printed Inman's reply, which once again was to decline the support of the paper for this position.[297]

In April 1896, after retiring from S. M. Inman & Company, Sam was visited by a committee of Atlantans that urged him strongly to consider running for the state senate for the fifth district, supposedly giving a number of reasons that were not reprinted in the paper that carried the story.[298] For a brief period of time, it appears that upon their request he decided to seek the office of state senator. From the capitol the announcement of his running met with favorable responses as reported by the same newspaper article.[299] According to a journalist, the support was due to "Mr. Inman's sterling personal qualities [which] are the pride of the entire community in which he lives."[300] Later that month he decided not to run, giving no reason. Even as late as 1913, Governor John M. Slaton, the brother-in-law of a niece's husband, offered him an appointed position in state government, but Sam gave his declining health as his reason for not accepting.[301]

The re-election of Alfred H. Colquitt as governor in 1880 is an example of the support Samuel M. Inman offered and reflected his influence. This election was contentious because of the controversy surrounding the resignation of General John B. Gordon from the United Sates Senate and Colquitt's appointment of ex-Governor Joseph E. Brown to fill this vacancy. Many political opponents of these three politicians, the so-called Bourbon triumvirate, and other citizens of the state felt that the government was filled with corruption, believing that the resignation of Gordon, the appointment of Brown, and the re-election Colquitt had been an arrangement among the three. The citizens revolted against the suspect developments, and to get Governor Colquitt re-elected took the support and effort of many of Georgia's leaders. At the Democratic convention in Atlanta in August 1880, Colquitt was not renominated by the convention delegates by a two-thirds majority but by a special resolution where the majority recommended him but the minority nominated former U.S. Senator Thomas M. Norwood. Considering the general feeling of distrust, which was apparent among the voters, a considerable amount of campaigning, promising, and persuading had to have taken place by supporters of Colquitt and Brown. Such supporters included Henry W. Grady, who organized and chaired the campaign committee, consisting of five members including Samuel M. Inman.[302] None of the records indicate the extent of Inman's role on the committee or his personal feelings regarding Colquitt, Brown or

Gordon. Perhaps it was the rhetoric and gentle persuasion, which convinced Sam to participate on the campaign committee, but it does appear that he supported Grady and the Bourbon ideas of the 1880s. Whatever his part, the end results of the committee was successful, and Colquitt won the election, beating Norwood 118,349 to 64,004.

Sam Inman may have declined opportunities to serve as mayor of Atlanta, governor of Georgia, or state senator, but he exerted political influence in the city in being a member of the city council. As a member of council in 1892, Sam was the head of the Cemetery Committee and led the effort to have a fence erected on the east side of Oakland Cemetery.[303] He was also a member of the board of education for the Sixth Ward during 1895–1897 and at the same time served on the public improvements committee for the city and the relief committee of the city.[304] Reflecting his interest in education and books, he was also a member of the board of education's standing committees on the library, on printing, on course of study, and on text books. Sam resigned his position with the Board of Education in the fall of 1896 when his brother, John, died, stating that he had been "away from Atlanta for some months and may probably be absent for an indefinite time."[305] Upon first receiving the resignation, the council decided that since he had been "such a great value to the city, and his public spirit, and the interest which he takes in all matters concerning the general good,"[306] they put the matter on hold, giving him an opportunity to withdraw his resignation. In later council minutes, Mayor Porter King stressed the regret with which they complied with his request.[307] Not only did he serve the city in these various council positions, but he was also on the committee that drew up a new constitution and by-laws for the reorganization of the Chamber of Commerce in May 1883.[308]

Although these positions were not particularly powerful and they did not go for an extended period of time, it is a testament to Sam Inman's prominence that upon hearing of his death, the county courts and United States District Court adjourned for the day, the flags over City Hall were flown at half-mast, and the Atlanta Chamber of Commerce unanimously adopted resolutions asking that all businesses close their doors for an hour during the funeral.[309] At the funeral a special section was reserved for Mayor James G. Woodward, the city council members, and the Chamber of Commerce delegation of fifty.[310]

Although Samuel M. Inman was a member of city council these few times mentioned, it was his brother, Hugh T. Inman, who played a more active role in the city government and served as a member of the city council. As far as the position of mayor, he considered running in 1904 but decided against it.[311] Although he never held the position of mayor, Hugh served the city and contributed to it significantly in other positions. He was a councilman for the sixth ward in 1889–1890, 1895–1896[312] and 1905–1906,[313] and from 1903 to 1905 he was an alderman for the sixth ward as well.[314] During his term as councilman in 1889–1890, he wrote the annual reports of the tax committee, the market committee, the manufacturing and statistics committee, and the legislature committee, all of which he was a member.[315] Although his name does not appear with the final reports, during his term as councilman in 1895 and 1896, Hugh was a member of the manufactures, statistics, freight rates and transportation committee. During this same term he served on the cemetery committee that oversaw the building a 2,600 foot wall for Oakland Cemetery and an entrance for it,[316] and he served on the prisons committee, the public improvements committee, the sanitary committee,[317] and in 1895 he served on the relief committee.[318]

Beginning in 1892, Hugh was the chairman of the finance committee of the city council, displaying a great interest in the finances of the city and a determination to manage the city, as he would run his own businesses.[319] He held this position in 1895, 1896, and 1904.[320] In his report of 1895, Hugh stated that the office stood as "a bulwark against jobbery and wasteful expenditures of public money, and should not be tinkered with nor changed in its financial provisions by hasty legislation"[321] indicating the importance he placed in the role he was playing. His colleagues referred to him as "the ever vigilant chairman" of the finance committee.[322]

Once, the city proposed a new water pump system for the water-works, which would cost between $100,000 and $200,000. Legal difficulties developed over the question of whether one city council could bind a succeeding city council to the specific terms of the contract. This legal problem threatened a delay in construction that would have denied the city clean water and perhaps impaired the health of the community. Hugh was determined that the pump be bought that he turned to the city attorney, William P. Hill, and reportedly said, "There is no law to prevent me from buying a pump if I want a pump, and I'll buy this pump myself and take my chances of getting the money back from future councils."[323] The quote comes from a glorification publication, which in typical fashion of the biographies of nineteenth-century men focused on their supposedly heroic acts. We do know that the offer was so unusual that an investigation was opened to see whether Inman might be acting as the agent for a construction company or if he stood to benefit from the construction of the water pump in other ways. The investigation did not find him connected with the firm hired to do the work or discover any conflicts of interest, and Alderman James L. Key offered to endorse Hugh's notes if the contractors felt it was necessary.[324] The city did get its new water tower, but it appears that the city council raised the necessary funds in order to purchase it, therefore declining Hugh's unusual offer.

Hugh's contributions to the city did not stop there. He even made the city a beneficiary in his will, leaving it 250 shares of preferred stock in the *Atlanta Constitution*.[325]

Following in his father's footsteps as a political servant, Edward, Hugh's son, had strong views on how local government should operate.[326] In order to express these views and to act upon them, he was a city councilman for the eighth ward in 1915–1916 and 1924–1925,[327] and he was a member of the Fulton County Board of Commissioners at the time of his death in 1931, serving as the chair of the finance committee.[328] Edward also served on the Board of Police Commission for the eighth ward, being elected by the city council in 1917 for a three-year period.[329]

Other committee members regarded him as "instrumental in passing a number of effective reform measures, including the reductions in the salaries of Fulton County department heads made each year."[330] The salary reductions were a measure taken during the depression to cut back on the expense of government. One of the more important roles Edward played in local government was in the merger of Fulton and Campbell counties, which was underway at the time of his death in 1931.

Before he held elected positions, Edward served the city as a member of the Chamber of Commerce, like all successful businessmen of his period. In August 1914, there was an economic emergency when it became difficult to get cotton to Europe due to the outbreak of World War I. The directors of the Chamber of Commerce met with several bankers from local banks in hopes of developing methods of dealing with the crisis. Edward H. Inman was a member of this committee, along with prominent Atlanta businessmen Robert F. Maddox, J. K. Ottley, Ernest Woodruff, Mell R. Wilkinson, W. S. Witham, A. P. Coles, T. K. Glenn, J. K. Orr, H. W. Miller, H. E. Watkins, Albert Howell, Jr., Frank Hawkins, Books Morgan, F. J. Paxon, Sam D. Jones and V. H. Kriegshaber.[331] The committee decided that the best way to handle the lack of currency, which was impeding the sale of cotton, was to ask the government to permit the banks to offer notes secured by cotton in warehouses, and they asked the federal government to deposit more money into Georgia banks in order to increase the supply of currency. This measure was adopted and implemented; allowing cotton, still a major cash crop, to be traded.

In regard of the office of mayor, there were some members of the Inman family that expressed an interest in acquiring it. As previously mentioned, Hugh toyed with the idea of running but did not. John W. Grant, son-in-law of Hugh T. Inman, considered running for mayor of Atlanta in 1910, but Hugh persuaded him not to run, fearing the additional load would be too much on top of his other duties. From a hospital bed Hugh wrote, "I trust you will consider well before making the race for Mayor."[332]   Apparently, friends had approached Grant or other supporters who wished him to seek the position, because Hugh stated "it is an honor the way the request [came] to you."[333] Of Grant's ability to serve the city, there was no question as far as Hugh was concerned; "as a citizen I would like to see you Mayor but as a friend the burden must be considered."[334] According to Hugh, it was the burden of the job that kept the incumbent mayor, Robert F. Maddox, from seeking re-election, although the law prohibiting a second consecutive term was changed in order to allow him to run.[335] For his interference, Hugh apologized for writing on such a topic, admitting that he was in no condition to be giving good advice, due to his health, and trusting that the advice would be received in the spirit it was written. Grant must have respected his father-in-law's concerns and felt they were valid because he never ran for mayor.

Edward H. Inman, Hugh's son, did seek the position of mayor of Atlanta, running with the encouragement and support of his friends, particularly the trustees of the Trust Company Bank of Georgia. According to the family he lost because he paid his entrance fees for the race and left the following morning with his family for their two-month European vacation, returning just before the election. According to Franklin M. Garrett, Edward H. Inman ran for mayor for the 1919–1920 term. The others interested in filling the position were James G. Woodward, James L. Key, and Dr. Louie N. Huff. Key won the most votes but not a majority, and a runoff between him and Inman, who came in second, was necessary. Inman withdrew from the race, because "Mr. Key was so nearly nominated in the primary that he really deserved victory" and "because I am persuaded a run-over for mayor is not for the best interests of this community."[336] Inman went on to say that he did not believe in the requirement that a successful candidate must receive a majority of all the votes cast in the primary.[337]

Other family members also served the city and county in similar capacities. Walker P. Inman was a member of the Fulton County Board of Commissioners in 1886[338] and a Commissioner of Roads and Revenues of Fulton County of several years.[339] Frank M. Inman issued bonds for the Atlanta schools during the 1920s and served as a member of the bond commission that built the Spring Street viaduct.[340] John W. Grant was a councilman from 1907–1909,[341] where he was chairman of the finance committee, and he was elected alderman of the sixth ward without opposition and served in this capacity from 1909 to 1911.[342] He was also on the Atlanta Board of Education.[343] The various positions these family members held, coupled with the more detailed ones mentioned, shows the community status the Inmans enjoyed and the numerous way in which they could influence the development of the city. Although they were looking out for their best interests, the city of Atlanta benefited in the end with improved streets, water pumps, sewers, and street lights, as well as increased industry and revenue.

Boosterism can take on many different forms. Perhaps one of the best examples of this is the boosters' involvement with the three expositions, which Atlanta sponsored in the two decades before the turn of the century. These expositions were, according to Don Doyle, "New South extravaganzas" because not only was the machinery and technology regarding cotton on display, but the expositions also focused on the people and leaders of the New South and displayed their wealth, mansions, ideas and attitudes.[344] This was an opportunity to show the world that Atlanta was not the Old South, with its old biases and loyalties, but was new, encouraging industry, and welcoming Northerners and foreigners to enjoy their wonderful city.

The International Cotton Exposition, the first of these expositions, took place from October 5 through December 3, 1881, in Oglethorpe Park. The city's leaders began to play around with the idea of having an exhibition in Atlanta, which would center on the state's number one industry, cotton. The idea of such an exhibition was new to Atlanta but common to larger cities. Atlanta first began to entertain the notion of an exhibit when it was proposed by a Northern economist, underwriter, and investor, Edward Atkinson of Boston, Massachusetts, whose interest was in the growth and production of cotton, not its manufacturing into cloth. Atkinson ran a letter in the *New York Herald* advising a discussion and demonstration of the gathering of cotton to be held in a Southern city, and Atkinson's letter was reprinted in the *Atlanta Constitution* on August 29, 1880. It was this letter that planted the seeds of the New South movement in Atlanta. Atlanta businessmen were interested in the idea, but they wanted more emphasis placed on the textile industry, and they were able to persuade Northern supporters that Atlanta was the best city in which to hold a cotton industry exhibit.

An exhibition of this type would bring the attention of the country to the New South, and the boosters wanted to make sure that the city took every advantage of this opportunity. Not only were they as businessmen going to benefit from the technology introduced regarding the production of cotton, but also the city would profit from the many visitors who would be coming there. National newspapers would cover this event. Many citizens, particularly those with investments in local businesses, hoped for a positive image of Atlanta. The cotton exposition would put Atlanta on the map nationally as the headquarters of the New South movement, a very desirable position as far as the business leaders were concerned. The exposition of 1881 had four purposes: to foster reconciliation of North and South, to encourage the adoption of better agricultural techniques, to acquire Northern industrial know-how, and to "promote Atlanta as an interior marketing center for cotton."[345]

Of course, Samuel M. Inman and the rest of the Inman family had a vested interest in the International Cotton Exposition of 1881. Any knowledge, which would enhance the quality and quantity of locally produced cotton or the manufacturing of cotton products, would be very beneficial to the Inmans' cotton businesses. Both Sam and John were instrumental in making the exposition happen; in order to insure the success of the International Cotton Exposition, Sam worked as the treasurer of the exposition company from its inception along with Joseph E. Brown and J. W. Ryckman.[346] Local businessmen pledged to buy more than $36,000 worth of stock, and businessmen in New York, Cincinnati, and Boston bought the rest. One of the New Yorkers who gave strong financial support to the exposition was John H. Inman, a member of the exposition's executive committee.[347] Some of the other members of the executive committee of the International Cotton Exposition were Hannibal I. Kimball, Benjamin E. Crane, Robert F. Maddox, William A. Moore, Lemuel P. Grant, philanthropist, Thomas G. Healey, builder of the Healey Building, Sidney Root, pioneer Atlanta merchant and railroad engineer, Richard Peters, a substantial land owner, and Evan P. Howell, editor-in-chief of the *Atlanta Constitution*. Not only was John's personal support valuable to the organization, but he also played a key role as their connection with the financial community of New York, which purchased a significant amount of stock in the company.[348] Of the New Yorkers who financially supported the company through the purchase of stock, most were connected with railroads that operated in the South or with cotton brokerage firms in the North.

The successful selling of these subscriptions was the product of the campaigning of Samuel M. Inman and Hannibal I. Kimball, a prominent businessman and a native of Maine who had arrived in Atlanta in 1867.[349] Kimball was a personal friend of Atkinson, and their joint support and close relationship helped get the idea of an exposition underway. Sam is credited as having played a pivotal role in raising nearly ninety percent of the money needed by the exposition through his own expertise and by advancing "thousands of dollars out of his own pocket."[350] Stock in the exposition was sold not only to citizens of Atlanta, but many of the largest buyers were railroads and other businesses. The purchases as published in the newspaper were: Louisville & Nashville Railroad Company, $5,000 Richmond and Danville Railroad Company, $2,500 East Tennessee, Virginia & Georgia Railroad Company, $2,000 Constitution Publishing Company, $500 S. M. Inman & Company, $1,000 S. M. Inman, $1,000 and W. D. Grant, $100.

The *Atlanta Constitution* called the exposition, which opened on October 5, 1881, a "New Era Dawning upon the South,"[351] reflected in the attendance of General William T. Sherman. There were a total of 1113 exhibits on view at the exposition, coming from all over America plus seven foreign countries. To encourage attendance, the admission fee was set at twenty-five cents and the Western and Atlantic Railroad lowered its passenger fares to one cent a mile. Beyond the usual exhibits, different days were set-aside for special occasions such as Governor's Day and Cotton Manufacturers Day. The funds raised by gate admissions amounted to $195,518, and free admissions worth approximately $94,520 were granted. The exposition was heralded a success financially, artistically and industrially, and most importantly it accomplished its original goal in bringing together cotton growers and mill owners for a greater understanding of the staple.

Many felt that it was the careful eye and guidance of Sam Inman that caused the exposition of 1881 to be such a huge success.[352] A letter written by an "Observer" to the editors of the *Atlanta Constitution* praised Samuel M. Inman for his support for the exposition, writing that "but for him and his noble generosities, no doubt but that the exposition might have been a failure."[353]

Following the success of the International Cotton Exposition of 1881, there was interest among the business leaders for another enterprise. The next exposition was sponsored by the Piedmont Exposition Company, which was formed in July 1887, with Samuel M. Inman as an officer of the company. In order to obtain land for this exposition, the Piedmont Exposition Company became tied to the Gentlemen's Driving Club, and together the two purchased the desired piece of land, present day Piedmont Park, and agreed to allow the exposition to use most of the land and then to turn over most of the land to the club. This partnership was logical since most of those interested in having another exposition were also members of the Gentlemen's Driving Club, and they would benefit from the new cotton technology and the world's spotlight.

A few things were different from the previous exposition. This time admission was doubled to fifty cents per person, and important visitors included President Grover Cleveland and the First Lady. The most striking difference is the movement away from the emphasis on cotton and the industry surrounding it. Although it was present, this exposition focused more on bringing people to Atlanta and entertaining them.

Obviously cotton was still very important to the economy of Atlanta and of the South and perhaps it was still the reason for the exposition, only now the backers wanted to attract more people. This could be why the newspaper advertisements for the exposition focused on the bicycle races and the art exhibit, two spectacles unrelated to the cotton industry.[354]

With the success of the Chicago World's Fair of 1893, Atlanta leaders proposed yet another exhibition. The Cotton States and International Exposition of 1895, which took several years to plan, was held in Piedmont Park. Grander than the previous ones, this exposition more resembled a world's fair complete with rides and representatives of many different nations. However, once again the official focus was on the textile industry and production of cotton. Although the idea was far from new at this time, credit for the idea for this particular exposition went to William A. Hemphill, business editor of the *Atlanta Constitution* and former mayor of Atlanta. He wrote an article for the paper regarding the exposition and the Chamber of Commerce worked out the details. Samuel M. Inman presided at the first meeting with three hundred businessmen present, resulting in the appointment of a committee of twenty-five.[355] Those holding positions as officers in the Cotton States and International Exposition included many of the city's most successful and influential businessmen such as William D. Grant, father of John W. Grant, Jack J. Spalding, a successful attorney, William A. Hemphill, former mayor of Atlanta and business manager of the *Atlanta Constitution*. The list of board of directors was another who's who and included Samuel M. Inman, Hugh T. Inman, Clark Howell, Robert J. Lowry, Livingston Mims, William D. Grant, Captain James W. English, Evan P. Howell, and Porter King, mayor of Atlanta. Sam served on the board of trustees oversaw this project and was the chairman of the Exposition Finance Committee.[356] Serving in the finance committee with Sam was William D. Grant, Harry M. Atkinson, Robert J. Lowry, and T. B. Neal. Hugh T. Inman was also a member of the board of directors and was a member of the Executive Committee, of which Captain James W. English was chair.[357]

Naming the exposition became a very important consideration because not only was the cotton industry being promoted, but the city also wished to establish trade with Central American and South American countries; hence the name, Cotton States and International Exposition.[358]

The Inman family's involvement went beyond Sam and beyond the men of the family. Sam's wife, Mildred Murphy McPheeters Inman, was the second vice president of the executive council of the Board of Lady Managers,[359] which was in charge of the Women's Department and the construction of the Women's Building. Many wives of directors also served as members of the Board of Lady Managers, although not all of them were wives of directors.[360] An excellent example of a manager who was not married to a director was Nettie Sergeant, principal of Girls' High School. The women made up twenty-seven committees, which were headed by different managers. Mildred led the Assignment of Space Committee that was responsible for dividing up the Women's Building into the various exhibits, instructional areas, and a children's daycare center for mothers visiting the exposition. The exposition marked a change in the roles of women from traditional and supporting places in religious institutions into a broader sphere of social influence and activity. The changing role of women during this time period will be addressed in chapter three of this study.

In the early days of planning, the exposition experienced financial difficulties, and Sam once again came to the rescue. Several months before the exposition opened, it needed $100,000 and Sam Inman headed the list of donors with a contribution of $20,000. A few months later, the exposition was in need of an additional $60,000, and Sam "started the ball to rolling by giving $10,000."[361] Inman made these donations and initiated a challenge to other Atlanta businessmen to do the same, and other businessmen met these challenges, whether out of honest support of the cause or simply for fear of being upstaged by Sam Inman. Whatever the case, this method raised large amounts of money for the exposition, and the city of Atlanta also provided an undisclosed sum, which was to be repaid in the following year.[362]

Atlanta's Cotton States and International Exposition in 1895 was significant beyond its attention to cotton. It was the first exposition of its kind to include an exhibition by and for blacks, which was necessary for funding from Congress.[363] Although it grew into a symbol of the new paternalism that existed at the time, a delegation of Atlanta's blacks brought forth the original idea. Boosters of Atlanta felt that advancement for African-Americans was essential before the South could progress. Perhaps this is why the exposition committee was willing to allow, and perhaps even encourage, black participation to some extent. Although Sam Inman endorsed the idea of allowing blacks to have their own building because they had implored him to help them, much of the support for a Negro building came from the federal government, and much of the success in getting the federal government to support the exposition financially was due to the appearance of three prominent African-Americans, Bishop Wesley J. Gaines of Georgia, Bishop Abraham Grant of Texas, both bishops in the African Methodist Episcopal Church, and Professor Booker T. Washington of Tuskegee Normal and Industrial Institute, on behalf of the event.[364] Washington, a speaker from the opening ceremonies, was the orator of the day. There was also a meeting of a black congress and a black women's congress at the exposition.[365]

Only a month after its opening, the Cotton States and International Exposition experienced financial difficulties and was threatened with bankruptcy. People were not attending as the trustees had hoped they would, and the exposition was losing money daily; the creditors demanded payments on the loans that they had made to the organizing committee. In order to save the exposition, Sam Inman stepped forth with a donation of $50,000 and once again he made a public challenge to other businessmen of the community to raise the other money. By the time the banks closed the next day, $94,000 more had been raised for the exposition.[366] These steps of saving the exposition and in turn saving the reputation of the city endeared Sam Inman to many people in Atlanta for the rest of his life. In his honor, Thanksgiving Day at the exposition was called Inman Day;[367] in addition, 50,000 souvenir tickets sold that day displayed his picture, one representing each dollar he donated to save it.[368] Because of the amount Sam Inman contributed on the three separate occasions, he was the largest individual subscriber to the company's original stock.[369] It was at this time that he received the informal title of First Citizen of Atlanta, which was associated with him until his death in 1915.

When it was over, the Cotton States and International Exposition had admitted 800,000 visitors, with 55,000 people present in Atlanta Day. The exposition had a total of 6000 exhibits and received international coverage with many of the stories having been written by the 3500 editors and writers who visited. Regarding the exposition, there were estimated to be 100,000 press releases within the year. This was a tremendous amount of coverage for Atlanta, now so closely associated with the cotton industry and the New South.

Once again in June 1906, the city leaders wanted to have another exposition. Sam was instrumental in persuading them to delay the raising of the needed $500,000 until later. Other former exposition boosters who spoke in favor of this delay were Hugh T. Inman, Captain James W. English, and Asa Candler.

Historians such as Don Doyle view the three cotton expositions as Atlanta's boldest display of industrial spirit and support.[370] The expositions brought to Atlanta the attention of those interested not only in cotton and the cotton industry, but also those interested in investing in other sections of the Atlanta economy as well. These acts of boosterism helped to advance the city as an industrial location for the twentieth century.

Samuel M. Inman's boosterism did not stop with politics and expositions, and it expanded as Atlanta grew. Many of his ventures paralleled the business interests of himself and his friends. The local newspapers, particularly the *Atlanta Constitution*, were some of strongest forums for propaganda, with editorials cheering each new enterprise launched in the city.[371] Henry Grady's leadership of the *Atlanta Constitution* surely led Sam to purchase a large amount of stock in the Constitution Publishing Company, since he and Grady were good friends and political allies. Sam bought into the company in 1888 by acquiring 100 shares of nonvoting stock from N. P. T. Finch.[372] Sam sold his shares of stock to the Bannigan estate sometime after Grady's death, from which Clark Howell, Jr. purchased them.[373] It was also through Sam's support that the family of Henry W. Grady was able to purchase their home following his death. Grady had suffered financial difficulties and had invested in cotton futures under the guidance of Sam Inman. However, the cotton futures did not do well, and Grady lost much of the money he had invested. Sam Inman felt obligated to Grady's widow and children following his death.

Hugh also owned a large number of shares in the *Atlanta Constitution*, which he had bought from Clark Howell, Sr. Hugh retained his shares in the paper until his own death in 1910, at which time he possessed a substantial amount of preferred and common stock.

The Inman family did not stop with the *Atlanta Constitution*. Walker P. Inman acquired control of the *Atlanta Journal* in the late 1890s, and the paper "claimed his warmest devotion" in the later years of his life.[374] The *Atlanta Journal*, established in 1883, had once been the New South sounding board of Hoke Smith, a future governor of Georgia. Under Smith the newspaper grew in circulation and expanded its coverage. Walker's role in the paper was not limited to controlling the stock because he even served as its president for a period of time. Neither a writer nor editor, Walker was very active in the newspaper's business, he provided it with financial support, and his contemporaries credited him with making it a success, retiring from active business in 1892. James Richard Gray, Walker's son-in-law, acquired Hoke Smith's portion of the paper in 1900, becoming general manager and editor. In 1905, he purchased controlling interest in the paper, which he held until his death in 1917. Under Gray the *Atlanta Journal* advanced into a well-read paper with what has been described as progressive ideas, including a page devoted to women and the dispatches of war. At his death his wife, Mary

Inman Gray, daughter of Walker P. Inman, assumed the responsibilities of chairman of the board of the *Atlanta Journal*, with her son working as editor-in-chief.

The Inman family's support of Henry W. Grady, the *Atlanta Constitution*, and later the *Atlanta Journal* are representative of boosterism in print, but they had investments in other businesses in Atlanta. They personally profited from endorsing their city as a place open to new industry, willing to lessen taxes on industries, and possessing a large blue-collar work force. These qualities needed to be publicized as a way of attracting new industries and Northern capital, and these duties were left to the able Henry W. Grady, editor and orator.[375] Henry W. Grady was the managing editor of the *Atlanta Constitution* beginning in 1880, after being with the paper for only four years, while Evan P. Howell was the editor-in-chief from 1876 to 1897. Historians have referred to Grady as Atlanta's best cheerleader and the paper was his megaphone. Grady was not personally committed to promoting the whole South, nor the entire state of Georgia; but he was dedicated to proclaiming Atlanta as the ideal location for new investment, and if the rest of Georgia and the South benefited from its success, that was all the better. Grady's objectives were local, clearly defined, and obtainable. Soon after the Civil War, the *Atlanta Constitution*, which was founded in 1868, ran articles, which were pro-business and pro-industry. Grady, who came to the paper in 1876, took charge of the campaign and made it a centerpiece of the New South movement of the 1880s.

Samuel M. Inman was a loyal friend and supporter of Henry W. Grady, accompanying him to several speaking engagements in the North. Whether it was his interest in boosting Atlanta or as a favor for his brother, John H. Inman played an important role in Henry W. Grady's success. It was John who arranged for him to speak before the New England Society of New York where Grady made his famous "New South" speech. The New England Society of New York was an organization of wealthy businessmen who could direct large sums of investment capital toward Atlanta. Many of the members of the organization were familiar

with Grady's journalism from his coverage of the Charleston earth-
quake.[376] This particular speech was very important in Henry W. Grady's
career as an orator, in the New South movement, and in the overall
impression of the South by the North. It marked an important turning
point in Grady's career because before this engagement, he had not made
a speech outside of Georgia.[377]

Grady, speaking to the organization at its December meeting in 1886,
developed the theme of the New South, and he was the perfect person
for the job. Although he was the son of a Confederate soldier killed in
battle, he himself had been too young to fight in the war, and he had
never been a politician. He was a member of the next generation of
Southerners, who gave the impression that they were self-made men not
dwelling on events from the past. Those attending the speech were the
leading businessmen of New York, and the list of the guests of honor
included John H. Inman, J. P. Morgan, Henry M. Flagler, Lyman Abbott,
Seth Thomas, Elihu Root, George H. Lincoln, Russell Sage, General
William T. Sherman, and F. Hopkinson Smith. Grady admitted to being
nervous since the New England Society of New York had never had a
Southern speaker and he had no idea how the society would receive him.
He was warmly received and his speech made a lasting impression on
many people. Undeniably, the speech was a success, one of the most
important any Atlantan has ever given.

Once again, the business leaders and elites of Atlanta were
promoting the city not only as the center of the cotton industry but also
as the center of the New South, complete with its forgetting of the Civil
War. Newspapers were the easiest way to influence the citizens, and daily
the newspapers informed the readers that Atlanta was reformed into a
modern city. Henry W. Grady was convinced that this was the best way to
build Atlanta, and he had the opportunity to take his support further
through speeches. Supporting, financially backing, and encouraging
Grady and his New South rhetoric were the Inmans. Grady served as a
catalyst, getting these ideas to the people from the leaders and busi-

nessmen who would immediately benefit from the recent change in ideology.

The Inmans not only led their community in times of peace and prosperity, but they were also instrumental in guiding Atlanta in the era of the First World War. The success of the American involvement in World War I was highly dependent on the cooperation of citizens, and it was the civic elites who were able to organize and motivate the population into accomplishing many of the government's requests. World War I was also very important to Southerners in particular because for the first time since the Civil War the South was able to show its patriotism toward the United States. A previous attempt to exhibit their support for the country during the Spanish-American War had not had the time to transpire into the magnitude it did during World War I. Much of this desire to disclose their willingness to help was directly related to the election of Woodrow Wilson to the presidency in 1912, since he was the first Southerner elected since before the Civil War. Wilson also held a particular fondness in the heart of Atlantans since he had been a lawyer here for a few years and had married a woman from Rome, Georgia.[378] Much of the support the elites of Atlanta gave the war effort was related to the fact that many of their sons were serving in the military, an often overlooked consequence that surely influenced the situation. The task of using this overwhelming display of patriotic pride was up to the various national, state and local organizations, which had to organize the individuals into manageable groups with clear direction.[379]

When the war broke out, everyone wanted to do his or her part, and members of the Inman family led the way. Edward H. Inman applied to the Army Air Corps, but the military told him that at the age of thirty-five he was too old for service. Instead, President Woodrow Wilson appointed him to the United States War Industries Board, where he was a member of the resources and conservation section. This consisted of a three-man panel, including Temple Gwathmey, president of the New York Cotton Exchange, and Will Clayton, of McFadden & Company. The council was in charge of allocating cotton to American allies and controlling its exportation.[380] He also served as a "dollar-a-year-man" on the War Finance Cooperation, making only a dollar a year for his service.[381] After the war, President Wilson appointed Edward to be one of three investigators to report on the place of cotton in the world economy. He traveled to England to discuss the creation of uniform cotton grades and prices between England and the United States.[382]

The Red Cross also received a significant amount of support from the Inman family. Edward served in a lesser capacity with the Red Cross. In May 1917 he was the chairman of rehabilitation following the fire, which had destroyed a large section of Atlanta. John W. Grant and Frank M. Inman were both on the finance committee with Frank as the chair of that committee, and both were on the citizens committee of the Red Cross in 1917. Frank was also vice chairman of the Atlanta Chapter of the Red Cross in 1917 and the director of Women's Work in the Red Cross that same year. During World War I, John was the business manager of the American Red Cross Sanitary Unit of Atlanta in the Department of Military Relief.[383] The sanitary training detachments were for the teaching of first aid, elementary hygiene and camp sanitation. The function of the Bureau of Sanitary Service was to secure sanitary control of the areas surrounding or adjacent to military bases.[384] Fort McPherson, near Atlanta, was such a location where these sanitary services were necessary.

Other family members did what they could in the war effort, holding various positions. For example, Hugh Richardson, son-in-law of Hugh T. Inman, served as a director for the state of Georgia during the United States Campaign for War Savings.[385]

The Inman women also played a major role in the war effort. Mildred McPheeters Inman was the chair of the Women's Council of National Defense, Georgia Division, an organization enabling women of each state to work together for national defense; she had been a member of the council since its creation. The organization was called upon to survey the present nursing resources, stimulate the interest of educated young women in nursing, increase hospital training school facilities, and secure suitable and dignified publicity.[386] In line with the purpose of the organization, Mildred wrote articles for the newspaper and the council's newsletter, giving instructions on what could be done in the Atlanta area toward the war effort. Her directions included preventing unnecessary waste, conserving foods, and safeguarding public health. She also encouraged people, particularly women, to become involved in a local Red Cross organization or to do child welfare work in their community. To achieve many of the goals set by the association, the Women's Council took some practical steps; first and most obvious, the council signed girls up for the United States Nurses' Reserve. It encouraged women to plant family gardens and to preserve fresh vegetables for later use, making more food available to feed civilians. The women also directed the gathering of nuts to help the Gas Division in its hunt for raw materials to use in the manufacturing of gas masks, which called for the highest grade of carbon, and nutshells contained the carbon necessary for the manufacturing of gas masks.[387] The council also called on the women of the state to make sure that every man who met the general requirement for the draft should register. How effective this particular request is impossible to determine, but it shows a call for a loyalty to the war effort over personal friendships.

Beyond the matter of health care issues, the association aided communities near training camps to organize their social and recreational resources to be of the greatest value to soldiers. This included making the soldiers feel at home and protecting them from exploitation. In order to achieve these measures, the community was to erect and maintain clubs and recreation facilities for the soldiers and make visits with relatives of the soldiers possible.[388]

Beyond her involvement with the Women's Council of National Defense, Georgia Division, Mildred was also appointed vice chair of the Georgia Council of National Defense, of which Governor Hugh Dorsey was chairman. Both of these organizations had similar goals, the Georgia Council being a subsidiary of the former organization. The difference between the two was that the Georgia Council of Defense had men and women working together in support of the war.

The American Red Cross, another banner around which elite women rallied, was closely tied to the Georgia Council of National Defense. Not only did they do much of the same work, but also the latter acted as a statewide clearinghouse for all women's work in order to eliminate duplication of effort. In its early years, the Red Cross operated on a completely volunteer basis.[389] The Atlanta Chapter of the American Red Cross was founded in 1914 and reorganized in 1916. Its success and rapid growth was due to the work of the Atlanta Federation of Women's Clubs, which ran an extensive membership campaign.[390]

Annie Inman Grant, daughter of Hugh T. Inman, was a leader in Red Cross work during the war.[391] In the American Red Cross, she filled many different roles both as an officer and as a worker. The finance committee, of which she was a member, had to approve all money spent for the purchase of supplies and other expenses in connection with the workroom, which was operated by the Surgical Dressings Committee.[392] Although her work with the finance committee was important, her greatest role with the Red Cross was as a member of the Women's Work Committee.

Women's work for the American Red Cross included a variety of activities, including packaging relief supplies such as surgical dressings, hospital garments, and other hospital supplies, making comfort kits, knitting sweaters and socks, maintaining canteen huts for traveling soldiers, assisting in all forms of civilian relief, assisting with clerical, stenographic and similar jobs, and packing Christmas gifts. Nearly 3,000 women in Atlanta and the surrounding area participated in the various roles from sewing and knitting to collecting periodicals, novels, and other books for the servicemen. This was the type of work that Annie oversaw, making sure that no detail was overlooked and that money was available to purchase the supplies that were needed.

Perhaps one of the most visible Red Cross activities in the line of women's work was the operation of the canteen huts, located where the soldiers were most likely stop to change trains. One was located in Inman Yard, while the other two for Atlanta were located by the Terminal Station and in the Seaboard Railroad yard.[393] Mrs. James L. Dickey served as the canteen chair and worked daily in the canteens along with her 320 devoted volunteers. The canteens were greeting posts from which the troops received food and visible support, which was good for morale. The canteens were very successful as far as the American Red Cross was concerned, greeting and serving more than 9,000 soldiers a month.

Many committees functioned under the education committee, offering classes in surgical dressings, elementary hygiene, home care of the sick, first aid, and dietetics. Not only did the classes focus on the war relief effort, but they also addressed the issues faced by civilians at home. Many of the classes offered in nursing helped alleviate the strain placed on the community when medical personnel went into military service.

On the education committee, Annie was responsible for explaining the purposes of the classes and for encouraging women to take them. Grades were assigned, and Annie explained the details of this process in her recurring article entitled "Women's Work," which she wrote for the Red Cross newsletter. Many of these articles were about knitting because people had many different styles of knitting, and the Red Cross wanted a particular kind of socks and sweaters made. Annie called for a person in each chapter to check over each item knitted or packaged by that chapter so that the division office would not have to carry so much of the responsibility. Often the items were knitted wrong, forcing the women of the state chapter to reknit them, a frustrating and time consuming process. Annie, along with her sister-in-law Emily and her sister Josephine, were just three of the women that were faced with this task, causing numerous letters and newsletter articles to be written on the subject. In January 1919, the Red Cross was calling for a halt in knitting, much to the joy of those overseeing the project, and Annie relayed the message to the chapters through the newsletter. Around the beginning of

April 1919, the Red Cross requested the chapters to knit, but this time it was for the refugee children throughout Europe.

As it grew dramatically, soon this division of the Red Cross needed more room. In April 1917, Annie donated the use of several rooms in the Kimball House for the period of the war, and the headquarters were moved.[394] The Capital City Club also contributed its entire second floor to serve as workrooms for the Red Cross. Here the surgical bandages were packed, first aid and nursing were taught, and the knitted items were stored until shipped.

After the war the headquarters were moved to 258 Peachtree Street. During World War II once again the chapter was in need of more space, and Josephine Inman Richardson offered the use of the old Hugh Richardson home at 840 West Peachtree Street.

By 1918, Annie was a department head and the director of the Bureau of Chapter Production, which no longer bore the title of women's division. The national organization honored her by appointing her to the National Women's Bureau,[395] apparently in appreciation for her help in finding space for the young chapter. Later Annie was the Director of Women's Activities on the executive staff.[396] At the beginning of June of 1919 Annie's position is no longer listed, and Annie does not appear to be involved any longer.

As a family, the Inmans were extensively involved in a multitude of roles in the war effort. The men used their financial knowledge and management capabilities to accomplish tasks assigned by the government or through volunteer organizations. The women took this opportunity to display many of their own talents in managing and directing finances and found a cause to which they could dedicate themselves and their time.

At the heart of the New South concept was economics. The idea of a New South involved the movement from an agrarian economy to one that was much more diversified and industrialized. Many of the concepts, which Grady boldly voiced in his speeches and wrote in his editorials, involved economic growth. His focus was Atlanta, and he strove to make Atlanta the pacesetter for the New South.[397] He was the spokesman for progressive Southerners and investors alike, and his ability to spread these ideas was due to men who not only supported him but also believed in the New South and invested heavily in it, such as Sam and John Inman. The New South movement slowly turned into the Progressive Era in the first decade of the twentieth century as the South advanced in industry and was ready to participate politically in the nation once again. This change is reflected in the South's support of World War I and the patriotic feelings, which were so prevalent during this period.

Atlanta has always been successful at boosterism. This boostering spirit was a powerful adhesive among the members of the business elites of the city, who formed a class of businessmen with a common interest, to advance the city and thereby to increase their fortunes.[398] They had a common goal, to make Atlanta the symbol of the New South. Immediately following Reconstruction the businessmen of the city joined forces with the journalists and with the politicians to push Atlanta into rapid expansion. Their desire to succeed as businessmen was directly related to their success as promoters of a city, which shortly before had been in ruins. Unlike Mobile and Charleston, Atlanta did not have the established social structure to prevent it from expanding into a great economic and industrial center, and the expansion of the city fed the desire for even greater growth.

Much of this growth translated into an expansion in the population. Migration of rural people into the urban areas was one way to expand the size of a city. Atlanta made itself attractive to immigrants by constructing industries and buildings, creating jobs, and improving streets and other municipal properties. Boosterism was not simply the promotion of a city through the press nor was it simply encouraging new industries to come; it included the development of things people looked for in a city. Many other things, such as education and religion, which made a city attractive, were also supported by the Inman family and will be dealt with in chapter 3.

The level of boosterism, which was necessary and desired by the business elites, could be obtained through organizations that served this purpose. Boosterism could be enhanced if one could also achieve an elected position on the city council, further entrenching one into the elite sphere of society. Perhaps the largest demonstration of boosterism in the history of the city was the three expositions, which put the whole New South on display.

3

THE INMANS AND
ATLANTA'S CIVIC CULTURE

---

erhaps one of the most important elements of life, civic culture,
was less changed by the New South rhetoric. The New South
brought in industry, encouraged foreign and Northern investment,
and changed the rhetoric regarding the Old South. These changes were
visible in business, industry, and even local politics, but how the New
South came to civic culture is harder to uncover, although, a change in
philosophy such as the New South had its effects in this realm as well.

The civic culture breaks down into three major parts, spiritual,
educational, and cultural, with smaller, closely related areas accompanying them. The same men who were heading or inspiring Grady's New
South lectures were leading the civic culture as great philanthropists.
The financial security they had achieved as businessmen of the New
South allowed them the opportunity to support more causes and institutions with a greater amount of money, but whether philanthropic
movements in Atlanta during this period arose from New South ideology
or were simply a continuation of paternalism from the Old South is hard
to determine. Perhaps the newest element in civic culture was the
changed role of women, who were able to venture outside of their homes
and church groups into social, cultural and even political activities.

Many of the philanthropists' causes centered around their belief that
men should help their fellow human beings, a result of the strong reli-

gious emphasis to which most of the leaders of Atlanta subscribed. This generosity was coupled with a Puritan work ethic, a common description of nineteenth-century men of power. From a strong Presbyterian background, the Inman family joined in this philanthropic crusade, which included bettering the city by supporting schools, churches, and cultural activities.

The importance of education was not lost on the many businessmen in the community who understood the need for professional training for members of their own class and the value of schooling for members of the working class. In the years after he retired, Samuel M. Inman spent most of his time and a large sum of money on institutions of higher education in the Atlanta area. He failed to finish his degree at Princeton when he left to join the Confederate Army, and after the war ended he felt that he was too old to go back to college. Always regretting not having completed his education, he continued to read the classics and pursue interests in other fields on his own. In his home he had an extensive library, which he enjoyed immensely and in which he took great pride, and most of the family's memories of Sam were of him in his library in the evenings reading.

In recognition of their achievements, the Board of Trustees of Princeton University gave diplomas to four members of the class of 1863 who did not graduate, and Sam was one of the four to receive this unusual award of merit.[399] Continuing in his connection of Princeton University, in 1913 he became the first president of the Princeton Alumni Association of Georgia and served two terms in this position. This love and appreciation for education went beyond Princeton, as he served as a member of the Rhodes Scholarship Committee of Selection for the state of Georgia and as a member of the Board of Education for the city of Atlanta.

The next generation of Inmans had a better opportunity to receive higher educations. Edward attended a college preparatory school in Lawrenceville, New Jersey, before enrolling in Princeton for two years; he was a member of the class of 1903 but did not graduate.[400] Hugh

Richardson, son-in-law of Hugh T. Inman, also attended Princeton.[401] His involvement with Princeton continued after he graduated, since he served as a trustee there as well as of Oglethorpe University in Atlanta.[402] After attending Boys' High School, Frank M. Inman attended the University of Virginia where he was a member of the class of 1895. John W. Grant attended the University of Georgia, where he was a classmate of his future brother-in-law, John M. Slaton. Grant furthered his education by attending the Eastman National Business College in Poughkeepse, New York, after graduating from the university.

The Inman women attended the finest boarding schools and finishing schools in the country. In the long tradition of appreciating the finer things in life, many of them received their education in the North, studying logic, French, voice and music.[403] Margaret J. Van Dyke Inman, wife of Hugh T. Inman, was educated at the Athens Female College in Athens, Tennessee, until the Civil War began, when the family moved to Quincy, Illinois, where she attended Asbury College.[404] Having received such an education, she made sure that her daughters were educated as well. Annie, Hugh's daughter, and Harriett, Walker's daughter, attended the Ballard Institute of Atlanta, and after graduation they roomed together at the Peebles and Thompson School in New York City where they attended with John's daughter, Lucy. One of Annie's daughters, Margaret, attended a boarding school in Baltimore, and the other one, Anne, attended a boarding school in Catonville, Maryland.[405] The other Inman women shared similar educational experiences with Josephine, Hugh's other daughter, attended boarding school in Baltimore. These were the typical educations received by elite women, focusing on traditional, classical classes for one or two years. It appears that only one of the women of the family, Mildred, Sam's second wife, received a degree from a college or university, and it was an honorary degree of doctor of law from the University of Georgia.

The level of education both sexes of Inmans had was very typical for Atlanta's elite at this time. There were numerous public and private schools in Atlanta serving them, with the females attending private schools and with the males attending Boys' High, a public school, after having been to private elementary schools. All of the children at some point went away for at least a year to receive some type of advanced education, often learning of new schools from prominent Atlantans who had sent their children there.

Beyond their own schooling, the Inmans, like other upper class Atlantans, sought to bring institutions of higher education to the city and to improve those that already existed. As a family, the Inmans' first educational endeavor was the Georgia School of Technology. Sam was considered to be a chief founder and one of the commissioners of this institution,[406] today known as the Georgia Institute of Technology. The first idea of such a school came about in 1882,[407] and historians credit Henry W. Grady with the original idea. He met with Sam Inman and others in Sam's office to discuss the idea of a school focusing on technology. They felt that for Atlanta to continue to grow it needed its own engineering school, which would provide a practical education. This desire for a technical school arose from the International Cotton Exposition of 1881 and the influence of Edward Atkinson.[408] The idea was that these young men would come to Atlanta to receive their educations and would stay there because they liked it so much; the city would benefit by having these engineers, and in time they would hasten economic development. No longer would the South have to depend on engineers from the North for their expertise. A school of this nature was obviously easy to support because of its potential for the city.

The supporters of the industrial school simply needed to persuade the state that Georgia needed such a school and that it should be built in Atlanta. Governor Henry D. McDaniel established a commission of men, one representing each town being considered. Samuel M. Inman was Atlanta's representative, and he was considered to be one of the most influential members of the commission.[409] In order to acquire the new industrial school, each community had to demonstrate its support, particularly financial support, of such an endeavor. Sam led Atlanta's bid by donating $5,000 for the foundation of the school and raising an additional $50,000 from the city, and $20,000 from private citizens, acquiring a site valued at $10,000, and making an addition annual pledge of $2,000 for twenty years, bringing the total bid to $120,000.[410] Much of the Inmans' support in having the technical school built in Atlanta could also be related to their desire for technical experts. As earlier noted, after the school was built the faculty and students helped keep the Inmans' mills in operation although it was financed in part by federal and state funds. Edward Atkinson, who was partially responsible for the school and who had encouraged the International Cotton Exposition of 1881, expressed his opinion and desire that the new industrial school be kept separate from the state university, the University of Georgia, and kept technical in nature, and Atlantans supporting the school agreed with Atkinson on these points.[411]

On the fourth ballot voting on the placement of the school, Atlanta received the necessary three votes from the commission and was named as the site on October 20, 1886, beating Athens, Macon, Milledgeville, and Penfield.[412] The site of the new school in Atlanta was at Peters Park. To further demonstrate Samuel M. Inman's role in the establishment of Georgia Tech and his ties to Henry W. Grady, the board of trustees voted to send Inman and Grady to Washington DC to request that an officer, who would oversee the early stages of the institute giving it a sound educational foundation, be assigned to the school.[413] The school was formally presented to the state on October 7, 1888, as the Georgia Institute of Technology, with Nellie Inman, Sam's daughter, present at the ceremonies to pull a lever to start the machines and open the doors to 130 students. Other Inmans also present at the opening ceremonies were Sam and Walker.[414] Support for the school did not stop there as Sam served as treasurer on the original Board of Trustees for eleven years and contributed to the school generously.[415] John W. Grant also served on the Board of Trustees for several years and was chairman. In 1913 he donated $15,000 for a football field named Grant Field in honor of his son, Hugh Inman Grant, who died of appendicitis at the age of eleven.[416] In 1920, Grant donated another $50,000 to end Tech's obligation to the

Peters Land Company for the acquisition of Peters Park.[417]   Another family connection, James Swann, partner of John H. Inman in Inman, Swann & Company, was also a major contributor to the Georgia Institute of Technology. There is a building on campus named in his honor.[418]

While the Georgia Institute of Technology was an all male school, Sam Inman was also eager to support higher education for women. He spent much of his time and money in helping develop Agnes Scott, the Presbyterian women's school in Decatur, Georgia. He served Agnes Scott Institute, today known as Agnes Scott College, in one form or another for over sixteen years.

The school was founded in 1889 under the initiative of Rev. Frank H. Gaines, pastor of the Decatur Presbyterian Church. He had a strong interest in education with a Christian emphasis for young women.[419] The Decatur Female Seminary was granted a charter in the summer of 1889, and it opened that fall with sixty-three students, three of them boarding, and four teachers. It was at the end of the first year of the Decatur Female Seminary that Colonel George W. Scott offered Dr. Gaines $40,000 to enable the school to find a permanent home. The only stipulation was that the school's name be changed in order to honor his mother, Agnes Irvine Scott. The trustees accepted this proposal, and the school's name was changed to Agnes Scott Institute.[420]

Five trustees, two elected from the members of the Decatur Presbyterian Church, two from the stockholders of the school, and the chairman of the board of the school, governed Agnes Scott College. Sam Inman's membership in the First Presbyterian Church of Atlanta gave him a closeness to the school, and his friendship with Colonel George W. Scott added to his devotion to it. Other family ties include Hugh, who was a business partner of Colonel George W. Scott in a fertilizer business venture.

Sam was elected a member of the Board of Trustees on February 3, 1899, and he was unanimously chosen to replace Colonel Scott, the chairman of the Board of Trustees, upon Scott's death in 1903. Although elected on October 15, 1903, he did not accept the position until

February 9, 1904, and held it until January 1, 1915, shortly before he died.[421]

During his years of service to Agnes Scott College, he made several major changes to the institution.[422] In 1901, he donated $5,000 toward the purchase of additional property, half of the total cost, enlarging the campus from nine to eighteen acres.[423] This was the first addition of property since the original gift of land from Colonel Scott and is the site of Rebekah Scott Hall.[424] In 1905, Sam's contribution of $15,000 toward the building of Rebekah Scott Hall was half of the total cost of the dormitory. Other family members contributing to the fund were Jane Inman with $1,000 and Frank M. Inman with $500. In 1909 Sam donated $50,000 necessary for the construction of a new dormitory named after his first wife, Jennie Dick Inman. Sam Inman also took credit for the building of the Carnegie Library and Lowry Science Hall, having been asked to approach Andrew Carnegie with a request for a donation for the building of a library. Other improvements involved the college physical plant, including a new boiler house, a deep well, a servants' house, and electric lights.[425] Beyond the physical changes, which were taking place at Agnes Scott College, scholastic changes occurred as well. Academically, Agnes Scott improved under his guidance, with the curriculum broadened and the number of faculty members increased.

In 1909, the General Education Board of the John D. Rockefeller Foundation offered the college $100,000 if the community would raise an addition $250,000. Sam led the campaign which was often referred to "as the first of the 'whirlwind' campaigns ever held in Atlanta"[426] by donating $50,000. Inman dorm came from this contribution. This was in addition to his previous gift of $25,000 and subsequent gift of $10,000 and it was through his efforts and assistance that the school was able to raise an endowment and extension fund of $350,000 from the public.[427] Along with these changes, the name was changed from Agnes Scott Institute to Agnes Scott College. Under the chairmanship of Inman, a preparatory school was established in 1906 in order to accommodate those young women not yet ready for college level work. The Agnes

Scott Preparatory School was short lived, and in 1912 under Inman's chairmanship the board of trustees voted to discontinue it in order to make room for the college.

Even though the endowment of the school was doubled under Inman, to $175,000 Agnes Scott College faced a number of difficulties. At the beginning of World War I, cotton prices dropped and college attendance fell. There was an outbreak of disease at Agnes Scott, and the school had to be closed for a period of time. To compound the problem, the college had acquired a debt of $50,000 in an effort to remain open. Sam offered $25,000 if the friends of the college would raise the rest of the amount and gave them six months to meet the challenge.

Many members of the upper class around the country felt that religious women were necessary for the country to continue to grow and prosper because it was the women who taught their children from a very early age the difference between right and wrong. Therefore, the women held the key to the future, and they should be educated in the various disciplines. Sam Inman followed this philosophy, demonstrated by his support of Agnes Scott College. After his death, the school published a dedication pamphlet which observed that Sam Inman's "interest, influence and leadership were largely responsible for placing [Agnes Scott College] among the foremost colleges for women in America."[428]

Agnes Scott College was dear to the hearts of other members of the Inman family as well. Mildred M. Inman, Walker P. Inman, and Frank M. Inman all served on the Board of Trustees of the school. Mildred was the first female trustee and served a life term from 1917–1947. Frank served from 1915–1950, and Walker from 1904–1905. Jane Inman made the school the beneficiary of her will; the $115,000 she left made up the Samuel M. Inman Endowment Fund and was to be used for educational purposes only.[429] After Sam's death, Mildred M. Inman continued to financially support Agnes Scott College as her husband had.

In 1902, leaders of the Presbyterian Church was looking to put a new college in the South, and a group of Atlanta citizens supported the Presbyterian University's coming to Atlanta. The president of the

Chamber of Commerce asked Sam Inman to lead the campaign to raise funds in support of the school.[430] Hugh T. Inman donated $5,000.[431] The movement failed due to lack of financial support and because of the terms of the agreement, which required two other institutions to merge with the new university.

Although most of the Inman family's support of education is reflected in the founding of the Georgia Institute of Technology, the continued leadership of Agnes Scott College, and the efforts to bring a Presbyterian university to Atlanta, there was another Presbyterian institution which also benefited from the financial support of Sam Inman. He was a large financial supporter of Oglethorpe University in Atlanta, giving $10,000 during the 1913 funding raising campaign,[432] and a member of its board. His grandson and namesake laid a cornerstone in an opening ceremony. At his death in 1915, he advanced $50,000 to Oglethorpe University for educational endeavors, and the board of trustees of the university adopted resolutions establishing a memorial professorship in his name.[433] There was support for Oglethorpe University from other family members as well. Hugh Richardson and Frank M. Inman were two contributors to the school,[434] and Hugh Richardson was also a trustee of the school.

Sam Inman had an interest in the education of African-Americans as well,[435] but his support for Atlanta University, an African-American college in Atlanta founded in 1865, was far less publicized. The African-American colleges in Atlanta were Atlanta University founded in 1865, Clark University founded in 1869, Morehouse College founded in 1879, Spelman College founded in 1881, and Morris Brown College founded also in 1881. Sam lent financial support to the university and also served on its Board of Trustees from 1883 to 1887.[436] Until 1887 all of Atlanta University's presidents and trustees were Caucasians. At the time of Inman's death the president of Atlanta University, Edward A. Ware, expressed the sentiment of the African-American community of Atlanta with this tribute: "Possibly some of Mr. Inman's nearest friends do not realize how wide a circle is affected by his death. He was a friend of the colored people in the best sense of the word, and they have suffered a deep loss in his death."[437]

Beyond serving on its board from 1883 to 1887, research does show his continued interest in the success of the institution. In May 1887, as a member of the board of trustees, Sam presided over the meeting in which the next president of the school was elected.[438] This would have been the election of the first black president of the school. His name also appears years later with that of seven other business leaders in March 1913 in a letter written to protest a plan that would have Atlanta University merge with Fisk University and move to Nashville.[439]

Not only was Sam Inman interested in higher education in Atlanta, but he was also concerned with the public education available in the state. He felt that the system could be more efficient, and he was instrumental in persuading the state in an increase of $500,000 in the annual appropriation for public education in Georgia. New buildings were provided for the state College of Agriculture, and eleven state district agricultural high schools were established.[440] To help support these improvements, private donations raised a little less than $500,000. In 1906–1907 under Governor Joseph M. Terrell, Sam headed the common school education cause, giving money to the same.[441]

In 1923 the city of Atlanta showed its appreciation for all that Samuel M. Inman had done for education in Atlanta by dedicating a school on Virginia Avenue in his memory and naming it after him.[442] It was a large school building for its time; three stories tall and accommodating 542 pupils. It cost $200,724.81 to purchase the land and to construct the building.[443]

Other schools also benefited from the Inmans' dedication to education. Louise Inman, Frank's wife, worked with Martha Berry in establishing the Berry Schools in Rome, Georgia. She raised money for the campus Mother's Building, which according to the Atlanta newspaper was the only memorial of its type to mothers in America.[444] Another school profiting from the Inmans' generosity was the Tallulah Falls School, which Mildred M. Inman supported financially and served as a trustee for several years.[445] Many of the women's organizations of Atlanta society, including the Colonial Dames of America, supported this school as well.[446]

Relations between black and white Atlantans changed in a number of ways around the turn of the twentieth century. Jim Crow laws began to appear before the turn of the century to insure separation of the races and to encourage white supremacy, while disfranchisement laws and white primaries, which were primaries that were open to whites only. Blacks were allowed to vote in the general elections, but since Georgia had a one party system, the elections were won in the primaries and the general elections were simply formalities.[447] This came close to eliminating the African–American vote. Tensions came to a climax in the Atlanta race riot of 1906.[448] Reports of African-American males attacking Caucasian females enraged members of the white community, who went into black neighborhoods to avenge these attacks and to ensure that they did not recur. Of these September events, which included lynchings and brutal beatings, John M. Slaton wrote to his wife a letter that began with the words "I am delighted that you and your Mother have not been here since Saturday night."[449] Of the situation Slaton said, "Conditions here would have disgraced darkest Russia. Occurrences here excited distrust in our people and their desire to enforce law and do justice. Mobs of hoodlums have murdered innocent Negroes without active interposition of authority."[450] From Slaton's letter the reader can sense the feelings Slaton has regarding the incident. If there were any question of his position, he later stated in the same letter that for the past two nights he had Dock, his father's servant, sleep in the room with him, while Bob, another family servant, had also stayed with him for protection, fearing to go home. Although his sentiment can be generalized to cover neither other members of the family nor others in his social class, Slaton wrote that John and Annie Grant had also allowed their house servants to stay at their house. Slaton ended this discussion of the race riots, putting his wife's mind at ease, stating that he thought "the situation [was] under control and peace [would] be restored in a few days."[451]

Although he was not a member of the riot committee that investigated the incident and made recommendations about how to prevent similar occurrences in the future, Sam had still more to say about the riot of 1906. When the committee released its report in January 1907, he wrote a letter to the editor of the *Atlanta Constitution* commending W. G. Cooper and George Muse, who were in charge of distributing funds for the victims of the riot. Of the report Sam stated that he had seldom "seen as brave or as just a report upon a delicate subject."[452] Not only did he feel that the funds were necessary, but he also thought that from this incident people should learn "to treat in a more just and kindly spirit those of the negro race."[453] Instead of questioning the initial issue of alleged attacks on white women by black men, Inman pointed out that the sins of a few were not to be used to punish the entire race. He believed that it was "wrong to stir up hatred and create prejudice against the negroes of our country because of a few."[454] Instead, he felt that "the great mass of the colored people of Georgia are hard-working, law-abiding citizens."[455] Of these people, Inman felt that if they got half the publicity received by those who broke the law the world would have a completely different view of black people, and he challenged the press to point out these people as representative of their race.[456]

For other reasons, the African-American population of Atlanta had a high regard for Sam Inman's brother Hugh. Richard D. Stinson, principal of the Atlanta Normal and Industrial Institute, sent a letter to the *Atlanta Georgian* after hearing of Hugh's death in 1910, expressing his respect. Having known him personally since Hugh had presided at an educational mass meeting in Turner Tabernacle in 1906, Stinson stated that he had "many reasons for saying he was a good man. I can say no more than that. I, with others, recall his wholesome, common sense advice."[457] Inman subscribed money to the Turner Tabernacle, donating $25 before the meeting and an additional $25 after he heard the congregation sing "On Jordan's Stormy Banks I Stand," which knowing the financial standing of Hugh Inman, was a minor amount but money that the Tabernacle appreciated nevertheless. Stinson also said that on several occasions Inman had told him "how my humble people with the proper education and sober, good sense in all things, right here could become good, honest and well to do by adjusting themselves to conditions and seeking to be good."[458] Much of this positive feeling among the African-American population appears also to have come from Hugh's treatment of his servants, about which Stinson commented, "I know of his good opinion and faith in a member of my race who had always been in his family."[459]

The *Atlanta Constitution* also printed a letter from Dr. Henry Hugh Proctor, pastor of the First Congregational Church, commenting on Hugh T. Inman's appeal among African Americans in Atlanta. The letter stated "the colored people together with the white feel that they have lost a real friend in the death of Mr. Hugh T. Inman."[460] Hugh helped African-Americans of Atlanta with his gift of "a thousand dollars for the completion of the mission house for the colored people on Fraser street."[461] Proctor also credited Hugh with giving generously to the Carter home for aged Negroes and to the African-American church on Houston Street. "In ways too delicate to mention here he showed himself a real friend to my people, and we sincerely mourn his loss."[462] These signs of support for the African-American community from Hugh may not have been as large as Sam's support of African-American educational institutions, but it should also be noted that Hugh was not a philanthropist on the same scale as Sam.

The religious convictions of Atlanta's business leaders were very important personal characteristics, mentioned in biographies and obituaries alike. For if men were lionized for their wealth and business success, and perhaps their shrewdness, they were no less praised for their honesty and religious convictions according to Don Doyle.[463] Their contemporaries saw them as self-made men even if they had inherited much of their fortune and believed them deserving of this good fortune, for they also had faced trials and had overcome obstacles through their own tenacity. Biographies, autobiographies, and obituaries emphasized those early setbacks, which all worthy men faced.[464] This form of flattery, referred to by Doyle as self-congratulatory, dominated the accounts of businessmen's lives in the Victorian period.[465] In their personal lives they were often driven by the Protestant work ethic, but their religious convictions also led them to efforts to help the less fortunate in the city. They believed that worldly wealth was a sign of a virtuous life;[466] when a rich man died, he might be praised as much for his self-denial, frugality and honesty as for his wealth whether he was known for those traits or not.

According to this regimen of virtues, perhaps the greatest and most noble occupation a man could have chosen was that of a minister. Before the Civil War, Samuel M. Inman is rumored to have desired to enter this profession, but as he worked with dying soldiers on the battlefield he had a change of heart. Although family members said that his faith in God was not weakened, they believed that he felt he could better help people by being a successful businessman instead of being a minister, for the more money he made the more he could accomplish through charitable contributions. Doyle sees Inman's desire to become a minister as a young man as being very important both as an insight into his personal values and as a justification for the money he donated to charities in Atlanta.[467]

The Inmans were devoted believers in Presbyterianism, and they practiced what their ministers preached by giving to charity, bettering their community and supporting causes that did the same. One such cause, over which battles were fought, was prohibition. It was one Protestant belief, which became a point of great debate in Atlanta, as well as across the South. Prohibition was a progressive reform and remained a powerful idea well into the 1920s.[468] In 1885 the Georgia legislature adopted a law allowing local elections on prohibition, and Fulton County became the first county in the state to petition for a vote under the new law. The forces divided into their respective groups with the wets wearing red badges and the dries wearing blue ones. Their arguments ranged from the evils of whiskey, particularly the creation of premature widows and orphans, to the damaging effects prohibition would have on such profitable businesses as the Kimball House bar.[469] Under the prohibition law of Fulton County, liquor was to be outlawed for two years and saloons had seven months before having to close. With the threat of a dry county, many of Atlanta's good citizens, women included, stocked up with alcohol for cooking and special occasions.

This controversial issue was one topic on which the *Atlanta Constitution* did not present a unified front. Henry W. Grady had remained uncommitted on the issue during the first round of debates and the election. Not known to be a drinker himself, Grady served alcohol to important visitors in his home. William A. Hemphill, business manager and treasurer of the Constitution Publishing Company, listened with Grady to the different sides of the argument, which flowed through their offices daily, and finally both came down on the side of the drys. Evan P. Howell, editor-in-chief of the *Atlanta Constitution,* was decidedly wet. Samuel M. Inman, owner of a block of nonvoting *Atlanta Constitution* stock and an influential businessman, was dry.

Prohibition returned to the election scene at the end of the two-year trial. This time the staff of the *Atlanta Constitution* did not keep their opinions to themselves. Howell led the wets in hoping to overturn the previous decision, and Judge George Hillyer, a recent mayor of Atlanta, and Grady, led the drys. Editorials of the paper, which were usually rallying points for the readers, remained silent on the issue; however, Hillyer and Grady were far from being quiet. As the second election approached, both of these gifted orators addressed large groups, gathering the dries for one last surge. Despite their attempts, the wets won in an allegedly fraudulent election, and the drys demanded a recall vote, among other things. Believing that the factionalism was getting out of hand, Grady called the other leaders of the dry movement to his office where he convinced them not to push for a recall election and not to support only dry candidates from now own, eliminating prohibition as a factor in local elections. Grady believed that the vote would come back to haunt the wets as they tried to enforce the provisions of the law and that the issue of prohibition was not important enough to divide the city.

In a letter printed in the *Atlanta Constitution*, Sam Inman endorsed Grady's advice to the dry forces.[470] With the support of such an influential businessman who was a leader in the community and a known advocate of prohibition, the issue was put aside for the well being of the city.

The Inmans' support for prohibition may have arisen from their religious convictions, and their sense of responsibility for the public morals of the city developed from their sense of their Christian duty. The root of their Christian beliefs came from their membership and support of the First Presbyterian Church of Atlanta, and they made substantial donations to it. In November 1861, Walker P. Inman and his wife Harriett became the first of their family to join this church. Shadrach W. Inman joined it in December 1865, together with his third wife and his youngest children;[471] Sam joined the First Presbyterian Church of Atlanta by letter on June 4, 1868;[472] Hugh and his wife, Margaret, joined the church in 1877, moving their letters from the First Presbyterian Church of Savannah. Both Sam and Hugh are honored by the church and their families with stained glass windows, created by Tiffany's of New York,[473] memorializing each of them; Hugh's window depicts "The Resurrection" and Sam's, "The Ascension."

The Inmans were active members of the church, serving in many different capacities. Sam was the Sabbath School Superintendent, elected in 1875, and Walker, Sam, and Hugh all were elders. Each also served on various committees, supporting the growth of the church and the community. For example, Hugh was a member of the day school committee, being appointed in 1886, and Walker P. Inman was a member and a ruling elder of the First Presbyterian Church of Atlanta and a senior officer at the time of his death.[474] First Presbyterian remained dear in the hearts of the family, and those family funerals, which were held in a church, were held there, including Samuel M. Inman's in 1915. The funerals of the other family members were held at their private homes with the pastor of the First Presbyterian Church presiding.

The second generation also did its part in supporting the First Presbyterian Church of Atlanta. John W. Grant was a trustee of the church, and Annie Inman Grant was the superintendent of the Sunday School for several years.[475] Edward was a trustee of the church, and Frank M. Inman and Hugh Richardson served the church as deacons.

The Inmans supported their church with their wealth. Hugh T. Inman often gave large sums of money to the church, and when a clerk of the church once stated to Hugh that Edward was a much larger donor than he, he got the response, "Edward has his father to support him, I don't!"[476] Hugh's largest gift was his contribution of $100,000 to the Southern Presbyterian Church for a fund to care for aged Presbyterian ministers and their families, provided that other contributors matched the funds with an additional $125,000.[477] The challenge was met, and the total amount of the fund reached $1,400,000. The care for aged Presbyterian ministers continued to be a favorite charity for the Inmans, as Walker P. Inman made the organization a beneficiary in his will and donated $5,000 to be used to purchase securities.[478]

Sam's contributions to the First Presbyterian Church of Atlanta included sending the ministers on trips to Europe.[479] Sam was also a major player in the construction of the new church building at the corner of Peachtree and 16th streets. He purchased a large corner lot on Peachtree Street for $46,400; and after the elders were convinced that the congregation would benefit from this new location, Sam sold this land to the church for the location of its new building. It is not clear whether Sam first purchased the land for this purpose and then persuaded the elders to relocate the church, or whether Sam profited financially from this transaction.

First Presbyterian Church of Atlanta also received numerous large donations from members of the Inman family in trust and wills. Jane Inman left the church with a gift of $5,000 at her death,[480] and Hugh T. Inman left the trustees of the church $10,000. The church also received $5,000 at Walker's death with which it was to purchase securities.[481]

Likewise the North Avenue Presbyterian Church in Atlanta also prospered from the Inmans' charitable contributions and support. The church itself owed quite a bit to Walker P. Inman for legend has it that it was at his home in 1898 that a group of Presbyterians met and founded the church.[482] Both of these Presbyterian churches received much assistance from the family members. In fact, there are also stained glass windows in the North Avenue church in memory or in honor of Hugh T. Inman and Samuel M. Inman. Frank M. Inman was an officer of North Avenue Presbyterian Church, and his wife, Louise Reese Inman, a member.[483]

Beyond their support of Presbyterian religious institutions, members of the family also supported pious causes of other denominations. The Tabernacle operated a hospital to which Hugh T. Inman donated $1000 in a response to a publicized report in which Dr. Len G. Broughton of the Tabernacle stated that he had received funds only from his own denomination, the Baptist.

The Inmans were obviously involved to a great extent with Presbyterian institutions of Atlanta. While they may have had political or business reasons for their church-related activities, the extent to which they participated in weekly church functions as deacons, elders, and Sunday School leaders does point to their having genuinely religious motives. The Inmans did follow a strict Presbyterian code in not allowing drinking, dancing or card playing in their homes nor in participating in such. These vices were discussed in letters Annie wrote her parents, Hugh and Margaret, from school, when she commented that dancing looked tiring and that she was glad that she did not engage in it.[484] However, by the time Annie's children were old enough, they were taking ballroom dancing lessons. Perhaps this is a reflection of Annie having married John W. Grant, a Methodist, who engaged in these pleasures, or in the general changing of society's expectations of people of elite status.

Perhaps the largest and most significant contribution Sam gave to a charitable organization was the gift of his home in Atlanta to be an orphanage run by the women of the First Presbyterian Church of Atlanta.

The women of the church had formed a ladies' aid society and had been providing for the orphans of the city for some time but had not had a building in which to care for them. The society had been working out of the Marietta Street Mission and had been attempting to raise money in order to build a small orphanage.[485]

Following the death of his first wife, Jennie D. Inman, Sam Inman offered their home on Peters Street to the society to be operated as a nondenominational orphanage;[486] The property included a large two-story house and spacious grounds, 120 feet by 310 feet, rent-free for ten years beginning October 1, 1892. Also included were the carpets, gas fixtures and other furniture in the house, and the other buildings on the property including the stables and outhouses.[487] Altogether the property was valued at $50,000. In addition, Sam contributed $2,500 a year to the support of the institution and paid the taxes and insurance on the property.[488] For this contribution, local journalists crowned Sam as Atlanta's "model citizen" in the *Atlanta Journal* and a "philanthropic" in the *Atlanta Constitution*.[489]

Sam Inman was not alone in his support of the orphanage, for it received the attention of the Atlanta City Council, which allowed it to have water free of cost.[490] As a member of the cemetery committee of the city council, Sam proposed that the city "donate a lot in Oakland Cemetery to the Managers of the Jennie D. Inman Orphanage."[491] At its next meeting the council approved the proposal, and in the following year an alderman's motion that a lot costing $100 in West View Cemetery be purchased for the orphanage was approved.[492] It is interesting that the lot was approved in West View Cemetery and not in Oakland Cemetery. In the fall of 1892, there was even an attempt by a member of city council's tax committee to exempt this piece of property from taxes as long as it was used as an orphanage.[493] This highly controversial measure was overturned in two years "because it [was] illegal and [set] a bad precedent."[494] The organization that ran the orphanage was a board of nine women, one from each of the leading churches in Atlanta. By May 1896, the orphanage had children available for adoption.[495] But it remained open for only five years,[496] closing because the women in charge did not meet Sam's conditions as to how the orphanage should be operated.[497] The orphans, white destitute children, were to be admitted until the home reached its capacity of twenty-five. If the orphanage was not at capacity for sixty days at anytime, the property was to revert to Sam or his heirs. The exact conditions he required have not been found or why they were not met, but the orphanage closed around 1901 and was rarely mentioned afterward.

Another organization, which received the support of the Inmans, was the Confederate Soldiers' Home. The movement to establish the home began in the spring of 1889 through newspaper articles written by Henry W. Grady in the *Atlanta Constitution*. Subscriptions totaling $30,000 were raised, and on May 8, 1889, the board of the Confederate Soldiers' Home held its first meeting. Grady was the president, and the directors were W. L. Calhoun, Amos Fox, R. D. Spalding, D. M. Bain, A. M. Foute, M. C. Kiser, and Samuel M. Inman. Having been a Confederate soldier himself, Sam not only served as a founding director of the Confederate Soldiers' Home, but also remained at this post until 1901,[498] when the home finally opened after many delays and setbacks.

Perhaps it was from his devotion to a past friend, Henry W. Grady that Sam also served on the board of trustees for the hospital named in Grady's honor. During the last years of his life, Grady was a strong advocate for establishing a municipal hospital.[499] After his death, others saw to it that a municipal hospital was built in his honor. Trustees laid the cornerstone in December 1890 and dedicated the hospital in May 1892 with an original capacity of 100 beds and ten rooms for paying patients. In 1896, the hospital added a children's ward and in 1903 a maternity ward. The hospital continued to grow through the turn of the century with the construction of a white patients' building and a pediatric clinic building providing service to children of both races.[500] On March 7, 1892, the board elected Sam, who had earlier been on the building committee, for a nine-year term on the first board of trustees for Grady Hospital.[501] He resigned the position in December 1897, while he was living in New York sorting out his brother's, John, financial and legal affairs.[502]

The hospital continued to gain the support of the Inman family as it grew and changed. Hugh T. Inman named Grady Hospital in his will as recipient of 100 shares of preferred stock in the Atlanta Ice & Coal Company.[503] Walker P. Inman also made the city's hospital a beneficiary at his death, donating $3,000 for the general hospital and $2,000 for the maternity ward.[504]

In the sphere of social charities Sam Inman gave to a variety of organizations, including the Young Men's Christian Association in Atlanta, where he provided a library.[505] Mildred also supported the YMCA, and the Girl Scouts of the USA received much of her attention as well. Other charities, which received the support of the Inmans, included the Atlanta Heart Association, a favorite charity of Emily M. Inman,[506] and a variety of smaller ones. During the Christmas season of 1930, Edward H. Inman sent the *Atlanta Georgian* his $200 county commissioner paycheck for the Empty Stocking Fund, mailing it directly to the editor and asking to remain anonymous.

Many of the successful organizations existing in Atlanta after the turn of the century were cultural in nature. If one's home city had an array of cultural institutions and events, then the citizens, particularly those who financially supported these institutions, enhanced their own reputation for refinement.[507] Such institutions and organizations in Atlanta benefited enormously from the support and generosity of the Inman family. Although elsewhere women often spearheaded such undertakings, in Atlanta more often than not it was their husbands who took leading positions, or at least lended their names in support. The only exception to this rule in the Inman family was Mildred M. Inman, the widow of Samuel M. Inman. She had the financial capacity to support many different cultural institutions and time to donate as an officer.

Members of the Inman family endorsed a number of cultural undertakings. The Atlanta Art Association, one of their pet projects, was established by charter in 1905 and soon after began to experience financial difficulties. In 1916, in order to help the organization and to stimulate local artists, Mildred Inman, who was a member, offered a $50 gold piece as a prize for an art contest.[508] She later served as president of the association, succeeding Robert C. Alston, and as a vice-president in 1926–1927 under President J. Carroll Payne.[509] Mildred was also a member of the Art Committee, to which she was appointed by the mayor, and worked with J. J. Haverty and J. Carroll Payne in Atlanta's bid for the Southern States Art League, a conglomerate of institutions and sources, which supported artists.[510] They were not successful in bringing the league to Atlanta.

Perhaps of all the Inman family members, John W. Grant was the most committed to the arts. The High Museum of Art, the Friends of Art, and the Atlanta Art Association received much of his time and support. Not only did he sustain these organizations financially, but he served them in active positions as well. In 1924, John was made the chairman of the finance committee of the Atlanta Art Association, a position he held for four years.[511] In 1927, he also served on the endowment subscription committee and on the executive committee of the Atlanta Art Association.[512]

Although John was a leader in the arts, other members of the Inman family also worked for the Atlanta Art Association. Edward served on the membership committee and on the board of directors during 1927.[513] By then the supporters of the Atlanta Art Association looked like a list of who's who in Atlanta's society and included: Edward and Emily Inman, Mildred M. Inman, Hugh and Josephine Richardson, John and Sarah Slaton, Henry and Roberta Inman, and Frank and Louise Inman.[514] The list of supports in 1928 was no less impressive, and a list of contributions also exist for this year and included: John W. Grant contributed $5,000 Edward H. Inman $1,000, Henry A. Inman $1,000, and Sarah F. Grant Slaton $500.[515] Many of these same people were on the board of directors that year also including John, Edward, Sarah and Mildred. Sarah Grant Slaton's ability to serve as an officer in this and in other organizations can be attributed to the fact that she had no children and to her husband's political status.

The most visible artistic endeavor in Atlanta was the High Museum of Art, named after Mrs. J. M. High and her two daughters, who donated property at 1032 Peachtree Street and gave financial support to the association. The High Museum of Art received much attention from the Inmans. John W. Grant, one of the museum's founders, along with his wife, Annie, contributed $5,000 during one of the fundraisers and was a member of the Friends of Art.[516] As a testament to Grant's influence, J. Carroll Payne, president of the Atlanta Art Association and the High Museum of Art for many years, wrote that it was most encouraging to him and others who had worked so long for the Art Association and the High Museum of Art that he now received letters from such prominent businessmen as Harrison Jones, John W. Grant, and Frank Lowenstein "in which they stress the importance of Art as applied to our commercial and cultural life."[517] One such letter he was referring to was from John W. Grant, which demonstrated the attitude of the Atlanta elite toward culture. "It is truly said that the progress, prosperity, and happiness of any city or community can be measured to a large extent by its appreciation and useful application of Art, and it is a strange fact that Art is very often usefully used without an appreciation, or even a consciousness, of its existence."[518] Art was yet another form of boosterism as it raised the community's level of refinement.

John W. Grant also helped organize the Atlanta Music Festival Association in 1908 and served on its first executive committee. Previously called the Atlanta Orchestra Association, after 1905 the organization was called the Atlanta Music Festival Association or the May-June Music Festival Association.[519] In the words of one historian, it established the "patronage of serious music and grand opera as a badge of upper-class culture in Atlanta."[520] The executive head was Colonel W. L. Peel, who along with his wife helped make Atlanta a center of musical culture. John W. Grant was a member of the executive committee from the beginning, a position he retained until 1922, and a director of the association in its early years.[521]

Perhaps the crowning glory of the Atlanta Music Festival Association was bringing New York Metropolitan Opera Company, with Enrico Caruso, to Atlanta in 1910.[522] In order for this to happen two hundred of Atlanta's leading citizens jointly pledged $40,000, which the company insisted on before it would journey to the city. In Atlanta, Caruso sang to a record audience of over seven thousand people in one night. The series of five performances attracted over 27,000 people. All of Atlanta's elite families had boxes at the opera, including John W. Grant, Edward H. Inman, Robert F. Maddox, Albert E. Thornton, Jack Spalding, Phinizy Calhoun, Forrest Adair, Eugene P. Black, Clark Howell, W. H. Kisers, J. W. Murphy, and Hugh Spalding.[523] John W. Grant was on the executive committee of the Atlanta Music Festival when it brought the Met to Atlanta.

Culture benefited greatly from the patronage and sponsorship of various members of the Inman family. Along with other elite families of Atlanta, they had traveled to New York and Europe, had visited many of the great cultural institutions of the world and returned to the city with hopes of creating similar institutions and organizations in their own city. The establishment of such institutions and organizations gave Atlanta the appearance of greater cultivation, and the patronage by elite families made them appear more cosmopolitan and refined as well.

Another part of culture in Atlanta was the various clubs supported by the elite. Private clubs were also municipal institutions because it was here that the members made deals which would result in the election of a new mayor, the passing of a tax exemption for certain industries, or the establishment of a new business; all of this might be done without any written record. Although political positions, corporate directorships, and wealth were necessary to make one a member of the elite class, these alone would not suffice.[524] In addition, one had to be accepted by the elite class as a peer, a step which became harder to achieve as Atlanta's social classes became better established and more exclusive. Often the line was drawn with exclusionary clubs, which depended either on one's ancestry or on one's ability to pay large amounts of money in membership dues.

It was during the early 1880s that the women of the elite class began to become involved with civic organizations.[525] Before this time, women who were able to leave their household chores to someone else involved themselves in church organizations and benevolent societies which strove to help those whom these women referred to as the "worthy poor." As women were able, thanks to the availability of inexpensive ready made products and cheap labor, to expand their interests beyond their own domestic sphere, the idea developed that women were responsible not only for moral homes but also for moral communities and towns.[526] The responsibility of these women was to transfer the principles of an efficient and well-maintained Christian home into the operations of the community, and the temperance movements were a direct result of this type of thinking.[527] For women who had household servants, giving them more free time, jobs and careers were not typically an option. Most of these women, a minority of the population and usually wives or daughters of substantial professional men, were able to use their energy and talents only in voluntary activities, or what has been referred to as "women's associational life."[528] This change for Southern women came from their involvement in the Cotton States and International Exposition of 1895, according to Doyle.[529] It was in this one event that women who had previously focused all their energy on religious charities opened their minds to new ideas, turning away from pure charities and toward other causes. One could also say that here the seeds of Southern feminism were sown, since Susan B. Anthony spoke to Atlanta women regarding the suffrage movement at this time.

The role of women in the Cotton States and International Exposition of 1895 was an outgrowth of the Columbian Exposition of 1893 in Chicago. It was at the Columbian Exposition of 1893 that women got their first opportunity to participate in a large, national celebration. Anne Firor Scott points out that perhaps the directors of the fair never intended for the women to take their part in the exposition so seriously. Yet the women took on the management of the Women's Building and oversaw the various exhibits and lectures that took place there. Surprising to many, the lectures were informative and thought-provoking on many issues facing women at the time, including long work hours, low pay, and children's health.[530] As isolated as this event may appear to have been, it actually drew upon the many different women's clubs around the nation and even spurred many into existence. Many elite women from Atlanta, including some of the Inman family, attended the Columbian Exposition of 1893 with their families, among them John and Annie Grant, who stopped in Chicago before returning to Atlanta from their wedding journey to Europe.[531] These women came back with the idea of a Women's Building and guest lecturers for the Cotton States and International Exposition of 1895, and more broadly with new ideas about the responsibilities women might undertake in their communities during this progressive era.

The Women's Building itself spoke for the new role women were to play in their society. Not only was it managed by women, but also the $35,000 needed for its construction was raised by women and the building designed by a woman. Women controlled the lectures and exhibits in the building and also managed the hospital and children's care center located there. These positions of responsibility were new to the women of Atlanta, but their success would send them into the next stage of development for their organizations and clubs.[532]

The Atlanta Women's Club, which was founded in 1896 and organized by many of the elite women of the city, was a direct product of women's involvement in the 1895 exposition. This organization was devoted to charity work and educational programs for the disadvantaged in Atlanta.[533] Other clubs also appeared about this time, some concerned with the cultural uplifting of the citizens of Atlanta, others strictly social. The 1900 Study Club and the Every Saturday Class for self-education assigned topics for research papers. The literary clubs were for women wanting to make up for the lack of a formal education or for women who wanted to learn more. One historian, Anne Firor Scott, associates these clubs with the large numbers of women needing to find paid employment.[534] Other organizations that had existed previously but received a boost from the new role women were playing outside the home were the Daughters of American Colonists, the Daughters of the American Revolution and the United Daughters of the Confederacy. Still other women's associations were dedicated to social uplift or community improvement, goals which later evolved into agitation for the right to vote.[535] Although there are no records of the Inman women's participation in the suffrage movement, Emily C. MacDougald Inman's mother was a leading suffragette in Atlanta, participating in various women's clubs, which supported the cause.

In the realm of clubs and charities, it was often the wives of the elite businessmen who took the initiative, and these organizations became a means by which they established their position among the social elite of the city.[536] Mildred M. Inman was more able than most women to participate in club activities and to support organizations financially because she was a widow with no children and she had money of her own to spend. She was a member of a number of organizations, like all the Inman women, including the Women's Club and the Georgia Federation of Women's Clubs, of which she was said to be a pillar.[537] The Georgia Federation of Women's Clubs consisted of five Atlanta Women's Clubs in 1896, Atlanta Women's Club, Every Saturday Class, Georgia Press Woman's Club, Nineteenth Century Class, and Reviewers Class. Atlanta City Federation of Women's Clubs consisted of seventy women's clubs of Atlanta by 1912.[538]

In social clubs, the women of the family were more active than their male counterparts because of the amount of time they could donate. One of the founding members and regents of the Atlanta Chapter of the Daughters of the American Revolution was Sarah F. Grant Slaton. Emily M. Inman was a member of the Colonial Dames of America,[539] her mother was first vice-president of the Young Women's Christian Association, and Annie M. Inman Grant an officer of the Committee of

Women of the Chamber of Commerce Expansion Campaign of 1920.[540] Mildred and Annie served the Nine O'Clock Club in many different capacities, including the greeting committee for General John J. Pershing, commander of the American Expeditionary Forces in World War I. Along with Mrs. Albert E. Thornton and Mrs. James L. Dickey, Mildred and Annie were chosen because of their dedication and service during the war.[541]

Beyond the clubs and organizations of women, there was one founded by men for the creation and maintenance of their elite status. Wealthy citizens of Atlanta enjoyed riding horses and driving carriages, and for many years there was ample space for these activities. But as Atlanta continued to grow and areas like Oglethorpe Park were taken over by industry, the need to establish a place for riding became apparent. The first organized effort for a riding club resulted in the Gentlemen's Driving Club. In 1887 an article ran in the *Atlanta Constitution* drumming up interest for a place where horse owners could go to enjoy the outdoors. Those supporting the club in this initial stage were Henry W. Grady, Joel Hurt, W. M. Dickson, W. S. Everett, A. W. Calhoun, John Keely, and Henry Jackson.[542] They acquired land for the club with the cooperation the Piedmont Exposition Company, directly tieing the members of the club to the second exposition held in Atlanta.

On September 14, 1887, the *Atlanta Constitution* listed the members of the Gentlemen's Driving Club. The roster included such businessmen and political leaders as George W. Adair, prominent real estate developer, Dr. James F. Alexander, William W. Austell, son of the late Alfred Austell, Rufus B. Bullock, Reconstruction Governor of Georgia, Patrick Calhoun, descendant of John C. Calhoun, J. S. Dozier, Laurent DeGive, owner and operator of the De Give Theater, W. W. Draper, Captain James W. English, former mayor and leading businessman, J. A. Fitten, William D. Grant, builder of the Atlanta and West Point Railroad and the Grant Building and father of John W. Grant, Henry W. Grady, managing editor of the *Atlanta Constitution,* W. A. Gregg, local hardware man, James R. Gray, editor of the *Atlanta Journal,* Aaron Haas, businessman, Evan P.

Howell, editor in chief of the *Atlanta Constitution*, Henry Jackson, M. C. Kiser, Robert J. Lowry, banker and councilman, Robert F. Maddox, former mayor, Livingston Mims, former mayor, Richard Peters, substantial land owner, Jack Spalding, attorney at law, Samuel M. Inman, William H. Inman, Walker P. Inman, and Hugh T. Inman.[543]

The Gentlemen's Driving Club received a new charter at the time of the Cotton States and International Exposition of 1895 and changed its name to the Piedmont Driving Club. Among the incorporators were Robert J. Lowry, Rufus B. Bullock, Porter King, Robert F. Maddox, Captain James W. English, Clark Howell, Livingston Mims and Hugh T. Inman.[544] Over the years all of the Inman men of Atlanta were members of the Piedmont Driving Club.

Hugh T. Inman was also involved in 1904 when the city was considering purchasing Piedmont Park from the Piedmont Park Exposition Company for $99,000.[545] He was one of a number of citizens and council members who spoke in favor of the purchase. Whether Inman was a shareholder of the Piedmont Park Exposition Company and stood to profit personally or whether he was looking out for the best interests of the Piedmont Driving Club in insuring that the area was not developed is hard to determine.

Another organization which local businessmen supported and frequented was the Capital City Club, founded in 1883; the Inman men were all members.[546] John W. Grant was a president of the Capital City Club in 1910–1912 and a member of the building committee, which erected the club's new facilities at the corner of Peachtree and Harris streets.[547] Edward H. Inman also served as president of the Capital City Club from 1915 to 1917.[548]

Other similar clubs also patronized by the Inmans included Frank M. Inman as a member of the Brookhaven Club of Atlanta, and Edward H. Inman as a member of the Druid Hills Golf Club of Atlanta, the Everglades Club of Palm Beach, and the New York Club.[549] Edward's memberships may not be typical of all the members of the family, but they do demonstrate his extensive traveling and his meeting of businessmen for many different parts of the country through clubs.

One of Edward's social activities, which led to his establishing the first car dealership in Atlanta, was his enjoyment of automobiles. As a driving enthusiast when cars appeared, he was the thirteenth person in Atlanta to receive an automobile license, dated June 30, 1904. Not only was he the president of the Fulton County Automobile Club, but his cars also won cups for various races such as the "Hill Climb" on Stewart Avenue, and he took participated in endurance tours and automobile races.[550] He won the endurance race from Atlanta to Macon for the big car division and also made runs to Jacksonville, Florida, and other cities around the Southeast. In 1909 Edward owned a six cylinder Stearns valued at $6,500 and a larger Stearns touring car valued at $5,700, which were considered by writers for the *Atlanta Journal* as the most valuable and fastest cars in Atlanta.[551] Both of these vehicles were destroyed by fire in 1909 while they were stored in a garage. Because of his love for cars, in November 1904 the city council elected Edward to be a member of the Board of Automobiles. Edward turned down this position two years later, citing the demands of his business.[552]

The Inmans held such positions in social and political spheres that they were asked to receive honored guests on the behalf of the city. Two of the most famous visitors they entertained were United States Presidents. Samuel M. Inman was one of the handful of businessmen sent to meet the train on which President Benjamin Harrison arrived,[553] and John and Annie Grant were members of the Capital City Club who received President-elect William Howard Taft to Atlanta.[554]

With their clubs and organizations, the elite of Atlanta created and validated their social standing in the city, and the Inmans participated in producing these clubs and organizations perhaps to help solidify their position. The clubs provided social functions for their members and also served as meeting places for the business leaders of Atlanta to come together and perhaps conduct business in an informal environment.

It was the family's support of local institutions such as colleges, churches, hospitals, orphanages, and clubs, which solidified the Inman family, men and women, in their social positions and gave them influence reaching into other spheres. Obviously, the money, which the family made in their businesses and industrial pursuits, enabled them to spend more of their time and efforts toward bettering their community. It was the Protestant work ethic that drove the male members of the family to achieve on a grand scale in their businesses. Yet, it was also this religious upbringing that led the Inman family to financially support programs to better conditions for those in need. They saw this as being their duty as Christians, not as councilmen; therefore, the support they gave charitable causes was done from a personal standpoint, often without acknowledgment. However, they were also businessmen and they were able to use their positions in city government to get special treatment for their businesses. They may have helped the city grow and provide more services for its citizens, but they also looked out for themselves and their interest.

Personal wealth was very important in the general social setting of the day for it was seen as a sign of reward for good virtue. To have wealth spoke of having high morals and of having lived life in such a way that a large reward was God's way of showing approval.[555] The Inmans had wealth, and they donated portions of their fortunes to causes, which they felt would help others. As the actual amount of wealth they amassed is unknown, the total amount of money they donated to the various charities is even harder to determine. After Hugh T. Inman died, his account books and records revealed the amount of money he had donated to charity, which had remained undisclosed from even his family until his death.[556] In 1889 it was declared that Atlanta had five men worth $1 million or more. Included in this count were Joseph E. Brown, William D. Grant, Edward Marsh, John Ryan and Hugh T. Inman.[557] How accurate this declaration is can not be determined. If it spoke to nothing else, it showed that other Atlantans felt that Hugh was one of its wealthiest men.

For his charitable contributions and focus on education, Sam could be referred to as a philanthropist in the style of Andrew Carnegie, feeling that the more money he had the more good he could do. His philanthropic tendencies were more focused on one town in a variety of causes instead of in many towns with one particular theme as the Carnegie libraries were. Inman's support of such a variety of Atlanta clubs, organizations, charities, churches and schools mirrored his diversification of his businesses, a contradiction to Carnegie's philosophy on investing as well. At his death in 1915, Sam Inman's public charity work was estimated at being one million dollars, and his private contributions could not be calculated although they were known to be numerous.[558]

In addition to Sam's charitable giving, the rest of the family also did their part in supporting the various foundations. As a group, the Inmans significantly influenced the development of Atlanta, creating some associations while providing others with necessary support. These institutions provided health care, education, religious guidance, and a sense of community.

CONCLUSION

The Inmans began their journey as displaced Southerners trying to regain the wealth and standard of living they had enjoyed before the Civil War. They acquired new interests and business skills along the way, achieving wealth beyond what they had enjoyed previously. The first chapter of this book examined the progression of the Inmans from cotton trading on their plantation to their vast business interests and investments, demonstrating their ability to adjust and diversify, to become partners with others in order to obtain their goals, and most importantly to acquire Northern capital to make it all happen.

The second chapter turned the focus from the private business dealings of the Inmans to their influence in the political sphere of the city, detailing their positions and roles with an emphasis on how these were used to benefit their own interests. Successful businesses are in successful cities so the focus turned to political roles to aid in the boosting of business. Boosterism of the city grew in the form of expositions and fairs.

The last chapter of this study showed how the family, after amassing their fortunes, turned to help the community through a variety of philanthropic causes. Since the Inman women were ladies of status, they did not visibly participate in the family businesses, explored in chapter 1, nor in the political arena, explored in chapter 2. However, they filled their roles as matrons of Atlanta, caring for others less fortunate and supporting education and cultural enterprises.

As the family traveled through these phases, which tended to overlap, the older members faded into the background while the younger generation took on the newer roles of leadership. Therefore, the first generation of Inmans was predominant because they were most important in their success in business. During the latter part of their business careers, the first generation began to take an active role in the municipal affairs and introduced the second generation to the same. When the second generation became the main focus, the family's wealth had been built up and their social positions had been solidified, leaving the second generation to build upon them but also to extend them in the area of charitable contributions and socially uplifting organizations. It is for this reason that the study's characters change slightly among the different phases, with perhaps only Samuel M. Inman illustrating in one life and career the layered dimensions of the family's history. The study continues through the end of World War I in order to illustrate the new role of the second generation, particularly of the women of the family as they come into more of a public role. A few future flashes occur throughout the book in order to inform the reader of other events that the Inmans would be a part of in the decade following World War I.

Of all of the details of business deals and political activities given here, the role elites played in developing Atlanta into the city it is today is evident, with the Inmans being an example. The Inmans were not unique, perhaps just persistent and lucky. They were successful businessmen who represented the New South and all the economic changes it encouraged. Perhaps one of the most important points to make about the Inmans is that they were not what many would consider typical Southerners, having clear loyalties to the Confederacy. Although they were Confederate veterans and contributed to the Confederate Soldiers' Home, there are no indications that they glorified the Old South, that they wrapped themselves in the Confederate flag, or that they wore the old patriotic gray and marched on Confederate Memorial Day. Instead, they turned their focus on the New South, turning their energy to rebuilding and encouraging new industries. In turn they began to focus more on the city around them; and as they retired from active business, they transferred their talents toward these other services. Their support of local hospitals, orphan homes, schools, and churches was another form of boosterism, which encouraged people to migrate to Atlanta and to enjoy these modern conveniences, which were not available in the rural regions.[559] These forms of encouragement increased the population, thereby enlarging the number of taxpayers and expanding the number of customers, all of which multiplied the wealth and status of business elites like the Inmans through the growth of the middle class.

This study is informed by the ideas presented by in *New Men, New Cities, New South: Atlanta, Nashville, Charleston, Mobile, 1860–1910*, with the Inman family serving as a test case for the various points of the Doyle's theory and used as an expansion of these. Doyle argues "that a business class took form in the cities of the New South as its leaders created a set of formal organizations that served their common interests, fostered a social affinity among themselves, and helped them form a common view of the goals they wanted to pursue for their cities, their region, and themselves."[560] These organizations include the Chamber of Commerce, various professional and business associations, social clubs, charities, and churches. Each of these organizations had related goals whose the end results were to solidify the wealth and social status of the elites. In Atlanta we see these so-called self-made businessmen taking every opportunity to boost the city, but the underlying reason was for their own economic advantage. This group above the general business elite created their positions in society with successful businesses, and then went a step further by participating in local government and cultural organizations.

SELECTED BIBLIOGRAPHY

Primary Sources

11th, 12th, 13th and 14th Semi-Annual Reports, (Combined.) of the Railroad Commission of the State of Georgia. Atlanta: Constitution Book and Job Office Print, 1886.
Agnes Scott College Broad of Trustees Minutes. Agnes Scott College.
American Red Cross. Atlanta Chapter. Atlanta History Center.
Annual Reports: City of Atlanta, 1889.
Annual Reports: City of Atlanta, 1890.
Annual Reports: City of Atlanta, 1895.
Annual Reports: City of Atlanta, 1896.
Annual Reports: City of Atlanta, 1905.
Atlanta Art Association. Atlanta History Center.
Atlanta City Council Minutes. Atlanta History Center.
Atlanta Music Festival Association Subject File. Atlanta History Center.
Colonial Dames of America. Atlanta Chapter. Atlanta History Center.
Exposition Cotton Mill Account Books. Atlanta History Center.
First Presbyterian Church of Atlanta. Records. Georgia Department of Archives and History.
Fulton County Court of Ordinary. Record of Wills. Georgia Department of Archives and History.
Fulton County Tax Digest. Atlanta History Center.
Fulton County Tax Records. Georgia Department of Archives and History.
Grant, John W. Personality File. Atlanta History Center.
Inman, Arthur Crew Collection. Atlanta History Center.
Inman, Edward H. Personality File. Atlanta History Center.
Inman, Emily Caroline MacDougald Personality File. Atlanta History Center.
Inman Genealogy File. Atlanta History Center.
Inman, Grant and Slaton Family Papers. Atlanta History Center.
Inman, Jane Walker. Personality File. Atlanta History Center.
Inman, Samuel Martin Personality File. Atlanta History Center.
Inman, Samuel Martin Scrapbook. Atlanta History Center.
Lumpkin, Kate Richardson Papers. Atlanta History Center.
Musical Association Papers. Georgia Department of Archives and History.

The Nineteenth Report of the Railroad Commission of Georgia. Atlanta: George W. Harrison, 1891.

Polk, R. L. *Atlanta City Directory for 1891.* Volume 15. Atlanta: Constitution Publishing Company, 1891.

Registry of Merchants. City of Atlanta Records. Atlanta History Center.

Scott, George W. File. Agnes Scott College.

The Seventeenth Report of the Railroad Commission of Georgia. Atlanta: W. J. Campbell, 1889.

Slaton-Grant Family Collection. Atlanta History Center.

Sherman, William T. *Memoirs of General William T. Sherman.* Volume 2. New York: D. Appleton and Company, 1875.

The Twentieth Report of the Railroad Commission of Georgia. Atlanta: George W. Harrison, 1892.

Secondary Sources

Adams, Myron W. *A History of Atlanta University.* Atlanta: Atlanta University Press, 1930.

"Agnes Scott College Bulletin." Memorial Number–Samuel Martin Inman. February 1915.

The Americana: A Universal Reference Library. Biographies. New York: Americana Corporation. 1933.

Atlanta Constitution.

Atlanta Georgian.

Atlanta Journal.

Atlanta: Yesterday, Today and Tomorrow.

Bacote, Clarence A. *The Story of Atlanta University: A Century of Service.* Atlanta: Atlanta University, 1969.

Billings, Dwight B. *Planters and the Making of a "New South": Class, Politics, and Development in North Carolina.* Chapel Hill: University of North Carolina, 1979.

Blicksilver, Jack. "The International Cotton Exposition of 1881 & Its Impact upon the Economic Development of Georgia." *Atlanta Economic Review* (June 1957).

Bryant, James C. Ph.D. *Capital City Club: The First One Hundred Years, 1883–1983.* Atlanta: Capital City Club, 1991.

The City Builder.

Coleman, Kenneth, et. al. *A History of Georgia.* Athens: University of Georgia Press, 1977.

Coleman, Kenneth. "The Georgia Gubernatorial Election of 1880." *Georgia Historical Quarterly* 25/1 (March 1941).

Commercial and Financial Chronicle.

Daily Post Appeal (Atlanta).

Davis, Harold E. *Henry Grady's New South: Atlanta, A Brave and Beautiful City.* Tuscaloosa: University of Alabama, 1990.

Deaton, Thomas Mashburn. "Atlanta During the Progressive Era." Ph.D. diss., University of Georgia, 1969.

Doyle, Don H. *New Men, New Cities, New South: Atlanta, Nashville, Charleston, Mobile, 1860–1910*. Chapel Hill: University of North Carolina Press, 1990.

Edge, Sarah Simms. *Joel Hurt & The Development of Atlanta*. Atlanta: Atlanta Historical Society, 1955.

Escott, Paul. *Many Excellent People: Power and Privilege in North Carolina, 1850–1900*. Chapel Hill: University of North Carolina, 1985.

Evening Sun (New York).

Garrett, Franklin M. *Atlanta and Environs: A Chronicle of Its People and Events*. Volume 1 and 2. New York: Lewis Historical Publishing Company, Inc., 1954.

General Catalogue of Atlanta University, 1867–1929. Atlanta: Atlanta University Press, 1929.

Howell, Clark, ed. *The Book of Georgia: A Work for Press Reference*. Atlanta: Georgia Biographical Association, 1920.

Hubbard, W. Hustace. *Cotton and the Cotton Market*. New York: D. Appleton and Company, 1923.

Hunt, Elizabeth. *American National Red Cross: Metropolitan Atlanta Chapter, 1914–1979*. Self published, 1979.

Klein, Maury. *The Great Richmond Terminal: A Study in Businessmen and Business Strategy*. Charlottesville: University Press of Virginia, 1970.

Knight, Lucian Lamar. *Reminiscences of Famous Georgians: Embracing Episodes & Incidents in the Lives of the Great Men of the State*. First Edition, Volume 1 and 2. Atlanta: Franklin-Turner Co., 1907.

Kuhn, Clifford M., Harlon E. Joye, and E. Bernard West. *Living Atlanta: An Oral History of the City, 1914–1948*. Athens: University of Georgia Press, 1990.

Maclachlan, Gretchen E. "Atlanta's Industrial Women, 1879–1920," *Atlanta History: A Journal of Georgia and the South* 36/4 (Winter 1993).

Martin, Harold H. *Atlanta and Environs: A Chronicle of Its People & Events. Years of Change & Challenge, 1940–1976*. Volume 3. Atlanta: Atlanta Historical Society, 1987.

Martin, Thomas H. *Atlanta and Its Builders: A Comprehensive History of the Gate City of the South*. Volume 2. Century Memorial Publishing Company, 1902.

McMath, Robert C. *Engineering the New South: Georgia Tech - 1885–1985*. Athens: University of Georgia Press, 1985.

McNair, Walter Edward. *Lest We Forget: An Account of Agnes Scott College*. Atlanta: Tucker-Castleberry Printing, Inc., 1983.

McPherson, James M. *Ordeal By Fire: The Civil War and Reconstruction*. New York: Alfred A. Knopf, 1982.

Memoirs of Georgia. Volume 1.

Moody, John. *The Railroad Builders: A Chronicle of the Welding of the States*. New Haven: Yale University Press, 1919.

New York Evening Post.

New York Sun.

Nixon, Raymond B. *Henry W. Grady: Spokesman of the New South*. New York: Alfred A. Knopf, 1943.

Notable Men of Atlanta. Atlanta: 1913.

Northen, William F., ed., *Men of Mark in Georgia*, Volume 4. Atlanta: A. B. Caldwell, 1908, 230.

Pioneer Citizens: History of Atlanta.

Reminiscences of Famous Georgians.

Roth, Darlene Rebecca. *Matronage: Patterns in Women's Organizations, Atlanta, Georgia, 1890–1940.* New York: Carlson Publishing, Inc., 1994.

Russell, James Michael. *Atlanta: 1840–1890; City Building in the Old South & the New.* Baton Rouge: Louisiana State University Press, 1988.

Savannah News.

Scott, Anne Firor. *Natural Allies: Women's Associations in American History.* Urbana: University of Illinois Press, 1992.

_____. *The Southern Lady: From Pedestal to Politics, 1830–1930.* Chicago: University of Chicago Press, 1970.

Shore, Laurence. *Southern Capitalists: The Ideological Leadership of an Elite, 1832–1885.* Chapel Hill: University of North Carolina Press, 1936.

Stover, John F. "Northern Financial Interests in Southern Railroads," *Georgia Historical Quarterly* 39/3 (1955).

_____. *The Railroads of the South, 1865–1900: A Study in Finance and Control.* Chapel Hill: University of North Carolina Press, 1955.

Tindall, George B. *The Emergence of the New South, 1913–1945.* Baton Rouge: Louisiana State University, 1967.

Virginia General Assembly, *The Code of Virginia.* Richmond, 1887.

Who Was Who in America: Historical Volume, 1607–1896. Revised Edition. Chicago: Marquis Who's Who, 1967.

Wiener, Jonathan M. *Social Origins of the New South: Alabama, 1860–1885.* Baton Rouge: Louisiana State University, 1978.

Williford, William Bailey. *Peachtree Street, Atlanta.* Athens: University of Georgia Press, 1962.

Woodman, Harold D. *King Cotton and His Retainers: Financing and Marketing the Cotton Crop of the South, 1800–1925.* Columbia: University of South Carolina Press, 1990.

Woodward, C. Vann. *Origins of the New South, 1877–1913.* Baton Rouge: Louisiana State University Press, 1971.

Appendix A

GENEAOLOGY CHARTS

These charts are arranged in order according to generations. Note on the second chart the placement of the female children is questionable. Mary and Elizabeth Inman must have been twins.

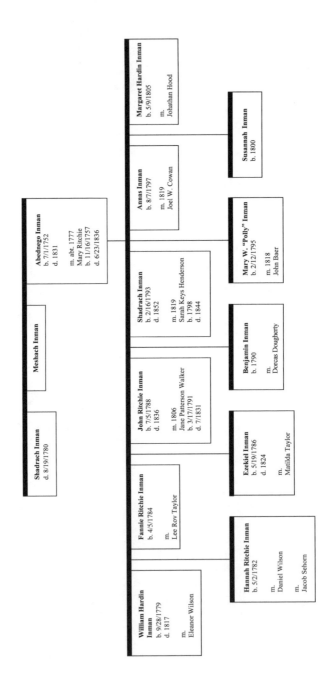

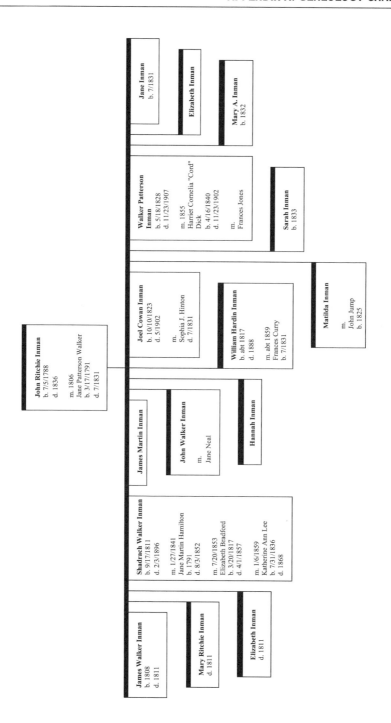

John Ritchie Inman
b. 7/5/1788
d. 1836

m. 1806
Jane Patterson Walker
b. 3/17/1791
d. 7/1831

Jane Inman
b. 7/1831

Elizabeth Inman

Mary A. Inman
b. 1832

Walker Patterson Inman
b. 5/18/1828
d. 11/23/1907

m. 1855
Harriet Cornelia "Cord" Dick
b. 4/16/1840
d. 11/23/1902

m.
Frances Jones

Sarah Inman
b. 1833

Joel Cowan Inman
b. 10/10/1823
d. 5/1902

m.
Sophia J. Hinton
d. 7/1831

William Hardin Inman
b. abt 1817
d. 1888

m. abt 1859
Frances Curry
b. 7/1831

Matilda Inman

m.
John Jump
b. 1825

James Martin Inman

John Walker Inman

m.
Jane Neal

Hannah Inman

Shadrach Walker Inman
b. 9/17/1811
d. 2/3/1896

m. 1/27/1841
Jane Martin Hamilton
b. 1791
d. 8/3/1852

m. 7/20/1853
Elizabeth Bradford
b. 3/20/1817
d. 4/1/1857

m. 1/6/1859
Katherine Ann Lee
b. 7/31/1836
d. 1868

James Walker Inman
b. 1808
d. 1811

Mary Ritchie Inman
d. 1811

Elizabeth Inman
d. 1811

145

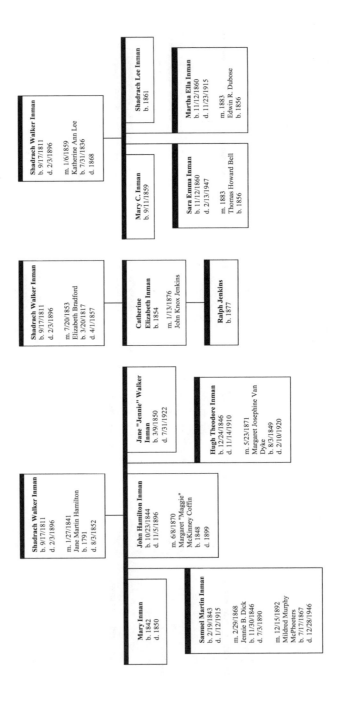

Shadrach Walker Inman
b. 9/17/1811
d. 2/3/1896

m. 1/6/1859
Katherine Ann Lee
b. 7/31/1836
d. 1868

Shadrach Lee Inman
b. 1861

Mary C. Inman
b. 9/11/1859

Sara Emma Inman
b. 11/12/1860
d. 2/13/1947

m. 1883
Thomas Howard Bell
b. 1856

Martha Ella Inman
b. 11/12/1860
d. 11/23/1915

m. 1883
Edwin R. Dubose
b. 1856

Shadrach Walker Inman
b. 9/17/1811
d. 2/3/1896

m. 7/20/1853
Elizabeth Bradford
b. 3/20/1817
d. 4/1/1857

Catherine Elizabeth Inman
b. 1854

m. 1/13/1876
John Knox Jenkins

Ralph Jenkins
b. 1877

Shadrach Walker Inman
b. 9/17/1811
d. 2/3/1896

m. 1/27/1841
Jane Martin Hamilton
b. 1791
d. 8/3/1852

John Hamilton Inman
b. 10/23/1844
d. 11/5/1896

m. 6/8/1870
Margaret "Maggie" McKinney Coffin
b. 1848
d. 1899

Jane "Jennie" Walker Inman
b. 3/9/1850
d. 7/31/1922

Hugh Theodore Inman
b. 12/24/1846
d. 11/14/1910

m. 5/23/1871
Margaret Josephine Van Dyke
b. 8/3/1849
d. 2/10/1920

Mary Inman
b. 1842
d. 1850

Samuel Martin Inman
b. 2/19/1843
d. 1/12/1915

m. 2/29/1868
Jennie B. Dick
b. 11/30/1846
d. 7/3/1890

m. 12/15/1892
Mildred Murphy McPheeters
b. 7/17/1867
d. 12/28/1946

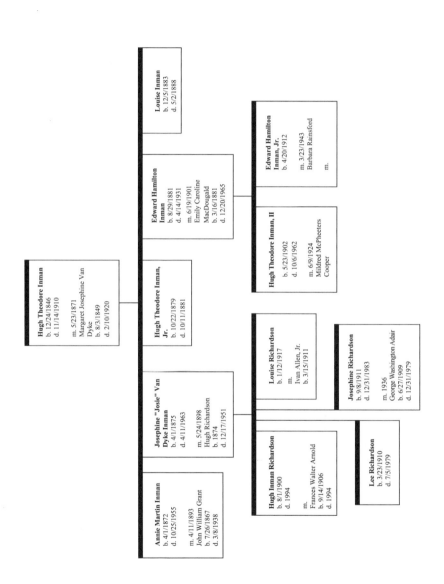

Hugh Theodore Inman
b. 12/24/1846
d. 11/14/1910

m. 5/23/1871
Margaret Josephine Van
Dyke
b. 8/3/1849
d. 2/10/1920

Louise Inman
b. 12/5/1883
d. 5/2/1888

**Edward Hamilton
Inman**
b. 8/29/1881
d. 4/4/1931

m. 6/19/1901
Emily Caroline
MacDougald
b. 3/16/1881
d. 12/20/1965

**Edward Hamilton
Inman, Jr.**
b. 4/20/1912

m. 3/23/1943
Barbara Rainsford

m.

**Hugh Theodore Inman,
Jr.**
b. 10/22/1879
d. 10/11/1881

Hugh Theodore Inman, II
b. 5/23/1902
d. 10/6/1962

m. 6/9/1924
Mildred McPheeters
Cooper

**Josephine "Josie" Van
Dyke Inman**
b. 4/1/1875
d. 4/11/1963

m. 5/24/1898
Hugh Richardson
b. 1874
d. 12/17/1951

Louise Richardson
b. 1/12/1917

m.
Ivan Allen, Jr.
b. 3/15/1911

Josephine Richardson
b. 9/8/1911
d. 12/31/1983

m. 1936
George Washington Adair
b. 6/27/1909
d. 12/31/1979

Annie Martin Inman
b. 4/1/1872
d. 10/25/1955

m. 4/11/1893
John William Grant
b. 7/26/1867
d. 3/8/1938

Hugh Inman Richardson
b. 8/1/1900
d. 1994

m.
Frances Walter Arnold
b. 9/14/1906
d. 1994

Lee Richardson
b. 3/23/1910
d. 7/5/1979

147

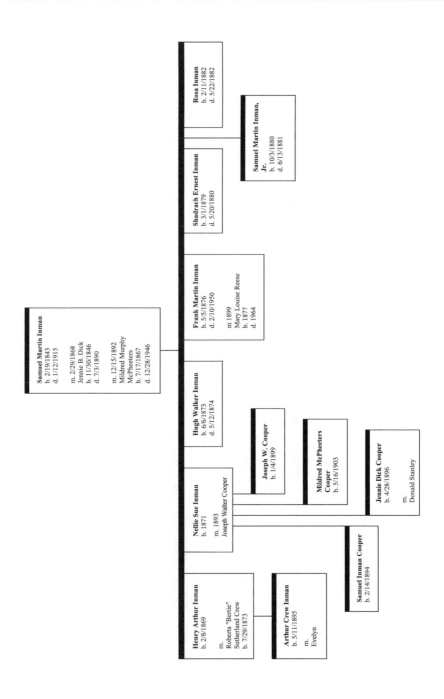

Samuel Martin Inman
b. 2/19/1843
d. 1/12/1915

m. 2/29/1868
Jennie B. Dick
b. 11/30/1846
d. 7/3/1890

m. 12/15/1892
Mildred Murphy
McPheeters
b. 7/17/1867
d. 12/28/1946

Rosa Inman
b. 2/11/1882
d. 5/22/1882

Samuel Martin Inman, Jr.
b. 10/3/1880
d. 6/13/1881

Shadrach Ernest Inman
b. 3/1/1879
d. 5/20/1880

Frank Martin Inman
b. 5/5/1876
d. 2/10/1950

m 1899
Mary Louise Reese
b. 1877
d. 1964

Hugh Walker Inman
b. 6/6/1873
d. 5/12/1874

Joseph W. Cooper
b. 1/4/1899

Mildred McPheeters Cooper
b. 5/16/1903

Jennie Dick Cooper
b. 4/28/1896

m.
Donald Stanley

Nellie Sue Inman
b. 1871

m. 1893
Joseph Walter Cooper

Samuel Inman Cooper
b. 2/14/1894

Henry Arthur Inman
b. 2/8/1869

m.
Roberta "Bertie"
Sutherland Crew
b. 7/29/1873

Arthur Crew Inman
b. 5/11/1895

m.
Evelyn

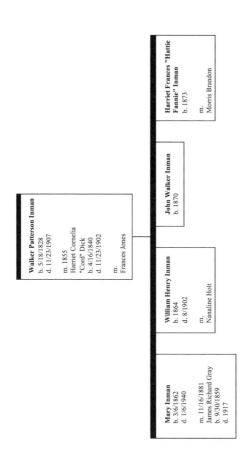

Walker Patterson Inman
b. 5/18/1828
d. 11/23/1907

m. 1855
Harriet Cornelia
"Cord" Dick
b. 4/16/1840
d. 11/23/1902

m.
Frances Jones

Mary Inman
b. 3/6/1862
d. 1/6/1940

m. 11/16/1881
James Richard Gray
b. 9/30/1859
d. 1917

William Henry Inman
b. 1864
d. 8/1902

m.
Nanaline Holt

John Walker Inman
b. 1870

Harriet Frances "Hattie
Fannie" Inman
b. 1873

m.
Morris Brandon

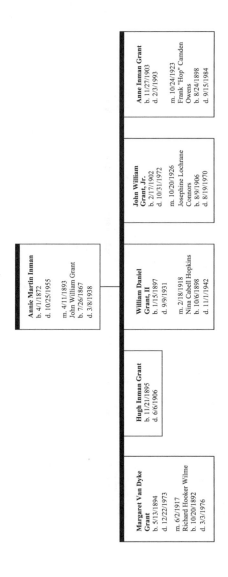

Annie Martin Inman
b. 4/1/1872
d. 10/25/1955

m. 4/11/1893
John William Grant
b. 7/26/1867
d. 3/8/1938

Margaret Van Dyke
Grant
b. 5/13/1894
d. 12/22/1973

m. 6/2/1917
Richard Hooker Wilme
b. 10/20/1892
d. 3/3/1976

Hugh Inman Grant
b. 11/21/1895
d. 6/6/1906

William Daniel
Grant, II
b. 1/15/1897
d. 9/9/1931

m. 2/18/1918
Nina Cabell Hopkins
b. 10/6/1898
d. 11/1/1942

John William
Grant, Jr.
b. 2/17/1902
d. 10/31/1972

m. 10/20/1926
Josephine Lochrane
Connors
b. 8/9/1906
d. 8/19/1970

Anne Inman Grant
b. 11/27/1903
d. 2/3/1993

m. 10/24/1923
Frank "Hop" Camden
Owens
b. 8/24/1898
d. 9/15/1984

Appendix B

RICHMOND TERMINAL SYSTEM

When John H. Inman resigned as president of the Richmond Terminal Company in March 1892, the Richmond and Danville Railroad Company was reaching the peak of its mileage. Records of June 1892 indicate the roads that were now subsidiaries of the Richmond and Danville Company and were being leased from 28 to 99 years but had not been officially bought out. They were as follows:

Asheville and Spartanburg Railroad Company
Charlotte, Columbia and Augusta Railroad Company
Atlantic, Tennessee and Ohio Railroad Company
Cheraw and Chester Railroad Company
Chester and Lenoir Railroad Company
Columbia and Greenville Railroad Company
Laurens Railway Company
Spartanburg, Union and Columbia Railroad Company
High Point, Randleman, Ashboro and Southern Railroad Company
Milton and Sutherlin Railroad Company
North Carolina Railroad Company
North Carolina Midland Railroad Company
Northwestern North Carolina Railroad Company
Oxford and Clarksville Railroad Company
Clarksville and North Carolina Railroad Company
Oxford and Henderson Railroad Company

Piedmont Railroad Company
Richmond and Mecklenburg Railroad Company
Richmond, York River and Chesapeake Railroad Company
State University Railroad Company
Statesville and Western Railroad Company
Virginia Midland Railway Company
Charlottesville and Rapidan Railroad Company
Franklin and Pittsylvania Railroad Company
Washington, Ohio and Western Railroad Company
Western North Carolina Railroad Company
Yadkin Railroad Company[1]

---

[1]Interstate Commerce Commission, *Fifth Annual Report on the Statistics of Railways in the United States for the Year Ending June 30, 1892.* Washington, 1893.

Appendix C

PHOTOGRAPHS

The following photographs are from
the Atlanta History Center's Library/Archives.

*Four Generations: Arthur Crew Inman, Henry Arthur Inman,
Samuel M. Inman, and Shadrach W. Inman*

Hugh T. Inman

Jennie D. Inman Orphanage

Samuel M. Inman

Edward H. Inman

John W. Grant

References

[1] James Michael Russell, *Atlanta, 1847–1890, City Building in the Old South and the New* (Baton Rouge: Louisiana State University Press, 1980) 105–107.

[2] Ibid., 92.

[3] Ibid., 92 and 108–109.

[4] Ibid., 113.

[5] Kenneth Coleman, et. al., *A History of Georgia* (Athens: University of Georgia Press, 1977) 201.

[6] Russell, *Atlanta*, 113–14.

[7] James M. McPherson, *Ordeal By Fire: The Civil War and Reconstruction* (New York: Alfred A. Knopf, 1982) 459.

[8] Russell, *Atlanta*, 113.

[9] William T. Sherman, *Memoirs of General William T. Sherman*, 2 vols. (New York: D. Appleton and Company, 1875) 2:178.

[10] Ibid., 2:180.

[11] Franklin M. Garrett, *Atlanta and Environs: A Chronicle of Its People and Events*, 4 vols. (New York: Lewis Historical Publishing Company, Inc., 1954) 1:427.

[12] Harold D. Woodman, *King Cotton and His Retainers: Financing and Marketing the Cotton Crop of the South, 1800–1925* (Columbia: University of South Carolina Press, 1968) 98.

[13] Ibid., 99.

[14] Russell, *Atlanta*, 125.

[15] Ibid., 123–24.

[16] C. Vann Woodward, *Origins of the New South, 1877–1913* (Baton Rouge: Louisiana State University Press, 1971) 116–17.

[17] Ibid., 119.

[18] Ibid., 29.

[19] Laurence Shore, *Southern Capitalists: The Ideological Leadership of an Elite, 1832–1885* (Chapel Hill: University of North Carolina Press, 1936) 161.

[20] Jonathan M. Wiener, *Social Origins of the New South: Alabama, 1860–1885* (Baton Rouge: Louisiana State University, 1978).

[21]Dwight B. Billings, *Planters and the Making of a "New South": Class, Politics, and Development in North Carolina* (Chapel Hill: University of North Carolina, 1979); Paul Escott, *Many Excellent People: Power and Privilege in North Carolina, 1850–1900* (Chapel Hill: University of North Carolina, 1985).

[22]Wiener, *Social Origins of the New South.*

[23]Escott, *Many Excellent People.*

[24]Russell, *Atlanta.*

[25]Shore, *Southern Capitalists,* 151.

[26]Ibid., 167.

[27]Don H. Doyle, *New Men, New Cities, New South: Atlanta, Nashville, Charleston, Mobile, 1860–1910* (Chapel Hill: University of North Carolina Press, 1990).

[28]Ibid., 89–92.

[29]Ibid., 137.

[30]Ibid., 93.

[31]Ibid., 17.

[32]Ibid., 19.

[33]Ibid., 18.

[34]Ibid., 17.

[35]Harold E. Davis, *Henry Grady's New South: Atlanta, A Brave & Beautiful City* (Tuscaloosa: University of Alabama Press, 1990) 46.

[36]*The Americana: A Universal Reference Library.* Biographies (New York: Americana Corporation, 1933).

[37]The old Inman home built in 1820 by Shadrach Inman, who is referred to as "Old Shade," is where President Polk and President Johnson were entertained. Shadrach Inman's son, William S. Inman, became the owner of the property and sold it to James Mitchell, who was its owner during the Civil War. It became known as the Mitchell House and later the Sheppard Inn.

[38]For more information on the genealogy of the Inman family refer to Appendix A.

[39]Woodman, *King Cotton,* 82.

[40]Will F. Inman, interview by Evelyn Yates Inman, 1926, Arthur Inman Collection, Atlanta History Center. (Hereafter referred to as AHC).

[41]*Atlanta Constitution,* 4 February 1896.

[42]Emma Mitchell Gass and Lon Mitchell, interview by Evelyn Yates Inman, 1926, Arthur Inman Collection, AHC.

[43]Dicy Bradford, interview by Evelyn Yates Inman, 1926, Arthur Inman Collection, AHC.

[44]Emma Mitchell Gass and Lon Mitchell, interview by Evelyn Yates Inman, 1926, Arthur Inman Collection, AHC.

[45]Ibid.

[46]Ibid.

[47]It appears that Shadrach retained ownership of some of the family land in Tennessee because he returned to Dandridge to live after the family's finances were stabilized.

[48]*Pioneer Citizens: History of Atlanta,* 138; Mrs. J.R. Gray, interview by Evelyn Yates Inman, 1926, Arthur C. Inman Collection, AHC. William F. Northen, ed., *Men of Mark in Georgia.* 7 vols. (Atlanta: A. B. Caldwell, 1908) 4:230.

[49]Atlanta, Fulton Co. Minutes Dr. 252, Box 44. First Presbyterian Church Records, Georgia Department of Archives and History, 17 November 1861 (Hereafter referred to as GDAH).

[50]Fulton County Tax Digest, AHC.

[51]*Daily Intelligencer*, 10 June 1863.

[52]Ibid., 25 March 1863.

[53]Fulton County Tax Digest, AHC.

[54]First Presbyterian Church of Atlanta Minutes, 2 December 1865, GDAH.

[55]Woodman, *King Cotton*, 305.

[56]Agnes Scott College Dedication Pamphlet, Samuel Martin Inman Personality File, AHC.

[57]Fulton County Tax Records, GDAH.

[58]Woodman, *King Cotton*, 247.

[59]Ibid., 246.

[60]Woodman, *King Cotton*.

[61]Ibid., 17 and 25.

[62]Ibid., 296.

[63]Russell, *Atlanta*, 154.

[64]*Atlanta Constitution*, 28 May 1892. Russell, *Atlanta*, 241.

[65]Doyle, *New Men*, 44, 103.

[66]*Atlanta Constitution*, 18 March 1891.

[67]Russell, *Atlanta*, 124.

[68]Ibid. Doyle, *New Men*, 44.

[69]Russell, *Atlanta*, 125.

[70]Doyle, *New Men*, 44.

[71]Agnes Scott College Dedication Pamphlet, Samuel Martin Inman Personality File, AHC.

[72]*Atlanta Constitution*, 13 January 1915.

[73]Ibid., 18 March 1891.

[74]Ibid., 13 March 1881.

[75]Maury Klein, *The Great Richmond Terminal: A Study in Businessmen and Business Strategy* (Charlottesville: University Press of Virginia, 1970) 39.

[76]*Atlanta Constitution*, 4 February 1896.

[77]W. Hustace Hubbard, *Cotton and the Cotton Market* (New York: D. Appleton and Company, 1923) 207.

[78]Woodman, *King Cotton*, 292.

[79]Ibid., 289.

[80]Hubbard, *Cotton*, 207–208.

[81]Henry A. Inman, interview by Evelyn Yates Inman, 1926, Arthur Crew Inman Collection, AHC.

[82]$122,689.17 in 1883 would be worth $2,111,601.22 in 2000. Samuel Martin Inman Scrapbook, AHC. In comparison, S. M. Inman & Company was showing an amount of $128,915.70 in October 1883.

[83]Edward H. Inman, interview by Evelyn Yates Inman, 1926, Arthur Crew Inman Collection, AHC.

[84]*Atlanta Constitution*, 15 October 1882.

[85]Samuel Martin Inman Scrapbook, AHC.

[86]*New York Evening Post*, 24 January 1882. Edward H. Inman, interview by Evelyn Yates Inman, 1926, Arthur Crew Inman Collection, AHC.

[87]Davis, *Henry Grady's New South*, 168.

[88]Garrett, *Atlanta and Environs*, 2:41.

[89]*Atlanta Constitution*, 3 March 1882.

[90]Russell, *Atlanta*, 235, 248–249.

[91]Ibid.

[92]Garrett, *Atlanta and Environs*, 2:42.

[93]Ibid.

[94]Gretchen E. Maclachlan, "Atlanta's Industrial Women, 1879–1920," *Atlanta History: A Journal of Georgia and the South* 36/4 (Winter 1993): 18. Russell, *Atlanta*, 249–250.

[95]Exposition Cotton Mill, Account Books, AHC.

[96]Russell, *Atlanta*, 125.

[97]Garrett, *Atlanta and Environs*, 2:412–414.

[98]Maclachlan, "Atlanta's Industrial Women," 18.

[99]Ibid.

[100]Thomas H. Martin, *Atlanta and Its Builders: A Comprehensive History of the Gate City of the South*, 2 vols. (Atlanta: Century Memorial Publishing Company, 1902) 2:384–85.

[101]*Atlanta Constitution*, 17 April 1931.

[102]*The City Builder*, Dec. 1923, 32–34.

[103]Doyle, *New Men*, 44.

[104]Registry of Merchants, City of Atlanta Records, 1871–1881, AHC.

[105]"Colonial George Washington Scott" Pamphlet, George W. Scott File, Agnes Scott College (Hereafter referred to as ASC).

[106]R. L. Polk, *Atlanta City Directory for 1891* (Atlanta: Constitution Publishing Company, 1891) 15:59.

[107]Morris Brandon, interview by Evelyn Yates Inman, 1926, Arthur Crew Inman Collection, AHC. Henry A. Inman, interview by Evelyn Yates Inman, 1926, Arthur Crew Inman Collection, AHC. *Atlanta Constitution*, 12 May 1897.

[108]*Atlanta Constitution*, 13 January 1915.

[109]*Successful Americans*, Samuel Martin Inman Scrapbook, AHC.

[110]Henry A. Inman, interview by Evelyn Yates Inman, 1926, Arthur Crew Inman Collection, AHC.

[111]Russell, *Atlanta*, 124.

[112]Klein, *The Great Richmond Terminal*, 14.

[113]Ibid.

[114]Lucian Lamar Knight, *Reminiscences of Famous Georgians: Embracing Episodes and Incidents in the Lives of the Great Men of the State*, 2 vols. (Atlanta: Franklin-Turner Co., 1907) 2:504.

[115]Klein, *The Great Richmond Terminal*, 38.

[116]Ibid., 90.

[117]Ibid., 93.

[118]John F. Stover, *The Railroads of the South, 1865–1900: A Study in Finance and Control* (Chapel Hill: University of North Carolina Press, 1955) 241. Ibid., 243.

[119]Klein, *The Great Richmond Terminal*, 105.

[120]Ibid., 45, 52–53.

[121]*The Seventeenth Report of the Railroad Commission of Georgia* (Atlanta: W. J. Campbell, State Printer, 1889) 3.

[122]Klein, *The Great Richmond Terminal*, 105–106.

[123]Ibid., 106–107.

[124]Ibid., 110–114.

[125]Ibid., 175.

[126]Ibid., 188.

[127]Ibid., 190.

[128]Ibid., 193.

[129]Ibid., 199.

[130]Ibid., 194.

[131]Ibid., 196.

[132]*The Seventeenth Report*, 38.

[133]Klein, *The Great Richmond Terminal*, 202.

[134]Stover, *Railroads*, 242 and 248.

[135]Klein, *The Great Richmond Terminal*, 202–204.

[136]Ibid., 35 and 196.

[137]Ibid., 39.

[138]*Atlanta Constitution*, 28 October 1888.

[139]Klein, *The Great Richmond Terminal*, 205.

[140]Ibid.

[141]Ibid, 205–206.

[142]Ibid., 206.

[143]Ibid., 207.

[144]Ibid., 209.

[145]Ibid., 208.

[146]Ibid.

[147]Ibid., 208–209. Stover, *Railroads*, 248–49.

[148]Klein, *The Great Richmond Terminal*, 209.

[149]Virginia General Assembly, *The Code of Virginia* (1887) chap. 47, sec. 1122.

[150]Klein, *The Great Richmond Terminal*, 212.

[151]Ibid., 232.

[152]*Atlanta Constitution*, 28 October 1888.

[153]Ibid.

[154]John F. Stover, "Northern Financial Interests in Southern Railroads," *Georgia Historical Quarterly* 39/3 (1955): 217.

[155]Klein, *The Great Richmond Terminal*, 236.

[156]Ibid.

[157]Stover, *Railroads*, 251.

[158]Ibid., 247.

[159]Ibid.

[160]*Commercial and Financial Chronicle* (12 March 1892): 443; (2 April 1892): 559–560; (16 April 1892): 643.

[161]*The Twentieth Report of the Railroad Commission of Georgia* (Atlanta: George W. Harrison, 1892) 18.

[162]*The Twentieth Report*, 17.

[163]Stover, *Railroads*, 250.

[164]Ibid.

[165]Klein, *The Great Richmond Terminal*, 14.

[166]Ibid., 240. Stover, *Railroads*, 251. Stover refers to him a Frederick P. Olcutt.

[167]Klein, *The Great Richmond Terminal*, 246.

[168]Stover, *Railroads*, 250–51. *Commercial and Financial Chronicle*, (26 November 1892): 895.

[169]*Commercial and Financial Chronicle* (26 November 1892): 895.

[170]John Moody, *The Railroad Builders: A Chronicle of the Welding of the States*, (New Haven: Yale University Press, 1919) 243.

[171]Ibid., 241.

[172]*Commercial and Financial Chronicle* 2 July 1892, 2.

[173]Ibid., 28 May 1892, 888.

[174]Ibid., 2 July 1892, 2.

[175]Ibid.

[176]*Commercial and Financial Chronicle* (6 August 1892): 216.

[177]Ibid., 27 August 1892, 332.

[178]Stover, *Railroads*, 252–53.

[179]Ibid.

[180]*Commercial and Financial Chronicle* (17 September 1892): 463.

[181]Ibid.

[182]Ibid., 24 December 1892, 1079.

[183]Klein, *The Great Richmond Terminal*, 255.

[184]Moody, *The Railroad Builders*, 188–89.

[185]Klein, *The Great Richmond Terminal*, 39.

[186]Doyle, *New Men*, 106 and 109.

[187]Woodward, *Origins of the New South*, 127.

[188]Klein, *The Great Richmond Terminal*, 39.

[189]Ibid., 15.

[190]*Atlanta Constitution*, 13 March 1881.

[191]Klein, *The Great Richmond Terminal*, 39.

[192]Stover, *Railroads*, 248.

[193]*Who Was Who in America: Historical Volume, 1607–1896,* rev. ed. (Chicago: Marquis Who's Who, 1967) 341.

[194]*Evening Sun* (New York), 15 November 1910. *Sun* (New York), 15 November 1910. John W. Grant to Annie M. Inman Grant, 21 October 1910, AHC, Inman, Grant and Slaton.

[195]*The Seventeenth Report,* 53.

[196]Atlanta City Council Minutes, 7 February 1891.

[197]Garrett, *Atlanta and Environs,* 2:240.

[198]Atlanta City Council Minutes, 12 February 1891.

[199]*Atlanta Journal,* 31 January 1883.

[200]*Atlanta Constitution,* 15 January 1915.

[201]Ibid.

[202]Ibid., 13 January 1915.

[203]*The City Builder* (December 1923): 32–34.

[204]*Atlanta Constitution,* 16 October 1904.

[205]Ibid.

[206]Ibid.

[207]Ibid.

[208]*Atlanta Journal,* 16 October 1912.

[209]Arthur Inman Collection, AHC. *The Seventeenth Report,* 57.

[210]Sarah Simms Edge, *Joel Hurt & the Development of Atlanta* (Atlanta: Atlanta Historical Society, 1955) 101.

[211]Doyle, *New Men,* 190.

[212]Ibid., 142.

[213]*Atlanta Constitution,* 16 October 1904.

[214]Edge, *Joel Hurt,* 73.

[215]Ibid., 196.

[216]Atlanta City Council Minutes, 6 July 1891, AHC.

[217]Ibid., 4 April 1892, AHC.

[218]Edge, *Joel Hurt,* 166.

[219]*Atlanta Journal,* 18 August 1897. Edge, *Joel Hurt,* 209.

[220]Garrett, *Atlanta and Environs,* 2:425.

[221]*Atlanta Constitution,* 19 August 1897.

[222]Garrett, *Atlanta and Environs,* 2:427.

[223]Doyle, *New Men,* 46.

[224]Edge, *Joel Hurt,* 77 and 79.

[225]Ibid.

[226]Ibid.

[227]Doyle, *New Men,* 46.

[228]John W. Grant Personality File, *Atlanta Constitution,* 9 March 1938, AHC.

[229]Klein, *The Great Richmond Terminal,* 39.

[230]Ibid., 106.

[231]Garrett, *Atlanta and Environs,* 2:514.

[232]Ibid., 1:685.

[233]*Commercial and Financial Chronicle* (15 November 1910).

[234]Garrett, *Atlanta and Environs*, 2:136.

[235]Edge, *Joel Hurt*, 264.

[236]Garrett, *Atlanta and Environs*, 2:191. Martin, *Atlanta and Its Builder*, 2:412. Northen, *Men of Mark*, 4:232. William Bailey Williford, *Peachtree Street, Atlanta* (Athens: University of Georgia Press, 1962) 88.

[237]*Atlanta Journal*, 10 February 1950.

[238]*Atlanta Constitution*, 17 April 1931.

[239]Garrett, *Atlanta and Environs*, 2:340.

[240]*Atlanta Constitution*, 9 March 1938. Garrett, *Atlanta and Environs*, 2:340.

[241]Woodman, *King Cotton*, 313.

[242]*Successful Americans*, Samuel Martin Inman Scrapbook, AHC.

[243]Walker P. Inman died in 1907.

[244]Garrett, *Atlanta and Environs*, 2:962.

[245]*The City Builder*, Dec. 1923, 32–34.

[246]Doyle, *New Men*, 195.

[247]Edge, *Joel Hurt*, 78.

[248]James C. Bryant, Ph.D., *Capital City Club: The First One Hundred Years, 1883–1983* (Atlanta: Capital City Club, 1991) 124.

[249]Russell, *Atlanta*, 236.

[250]Garrett, *Atlanta and Environs*, 2:60. Bryant, *Capital City Club*, 129.

[251]Inman Genealogy File, AHC.

[252]Bryant, *Capital City Club*, n. 1.

[253]Doyle, *New Men*, 196.

[254]Hugh Inman Richardson, interview by Jo Ann Warmack, 11 July 1976, Inman Genealogy File, AHC.

[255]Edward H. Inman, interview by Evelyn Yates Inman, 1926, Arthur Crew Inman Collection, AHC.

[256]Atlanta City Council Minutes, 6 July 1891, 15 February 1892, 7 May 1894, 16 October 1893, 4 June 1894, AHC.

[257]Inman Genealogy File, AHC.

[258]Inman, Grant and Slaton Family Papers, AHC.

[259]Edward H. Inman Personality File, AHC.

[260]*Atlanta Constitution*, 17 April 1931.

[261]*Atlanta Journal*, 10 February 1950.

[262]Klein, *The Great Richmond Terminal*, 39.

[263]Doyle, *New Men*, 102.

[264]Ibid., 101.

[265]Ibid., 219.

[266]Ibid.

[267]Ibid., xiv.

[268]Ibid., 101.

[269]Ibid., 18.

[270]Ibid.

[271]Ibid.

[272]Ibid., 19.

[273]Russell, *Atlanta*, 132.

[274]Ibid., 147.

[275]Woodman, *King Cotton*, 323.

[276]Russell, *Atlanta*, 148.

[277]*11th, 12th, 13th and 14th Semi-Annual Reports, (Combined.) of the Railroad Commission of the State of Georgia* (Atlanta: Constitution Book and Job Office Print, 1886) 6–7.

[278]Ibid., 7.

[279]Ibid., 13–14.

[280]*The Nineteenth Report of the Railroad Commission of Georgia* (Atlanta: George W. Harrison, 1891) 8.

[281]Garrett, *Atlanta and Environs*, 2:285.

[282]Clark Howell, ed., *The Book of Georgia: A Work for Press Reference* (Atlanta: Georgia Biographical Association, 1920) 553. Doyle, *New Men*, 148.

[283]Doyle, *New Men*, 148–150. Martin, *Atlanta and Its Builders*, 2:460.

[284]Russell, *Atlanta*, 131.

[285]Ibid., 170.

[286]Northen, *Men of Mark*, 4:231.

[287]Russell, *Atlanta*, 186.

[288]Ibid., 187.

[289]Ibid., 194.

[290]*Atlanta Constitution*, 12 October 1882.

[291]Ibid.

[292]Ibid., 13 October 1882.

[293]Ibid.

[294]Ibid.

[295]Ibid.

[296]*Daily Post Appeal* (Atlanta), 11 March 1883.

[297]Ibid., 12 March 1883.

[298]*Atlanta Journal*, 18 April 1896.

[299]Ibid.

[300]Ibid.

[301]*Atlanta Constitution*, 13 January 1915.

[302]Kenneth Coleman, "The Georgia Gubernatorial Election of 1880," *Georgia Historical Quarterly* 25/1 (March 1941).

[303]Atlanta City Council Minutes, 20 June 1892.

[304]Atlanta City Council, *Annual Reports: City of Atlanta, 1895*. Sam had replaced Hoke Smith, who resigned. Atlanta City Council Minutes, 7 August 1893.

[305]Atlanta City Council Minutes, 30 September 1896.

[306]Ibid., 5 October 1896.

[307]Ibid., 19 October 1896.

[308]Martin, *Atlanta and Its Builders*, 2:447.

[309]*Atlanta Constitution*, 13 January 1915.

[310]Ibid., 15 January 1915.

[311]Garrett, *Atlanta and Environs*, 2:352.

[312]*Annual Reports: City of Atlanta, 1896.*

[313]Garrett, *Atlanta and Environs*, 2:307.

[314]Thomas Mashburn Deaton, "Atlanta During the Progressive Era" (Ph.D. diss., University of Georgia, 1969) 458.

[315]*Annual Reports: City of Atlanta, 1889*, 28 and 47. *Annual Reports: City of Atlanta, 1890.*

[316]*Annual Reports: City of Atlanta, 1896*, 48–50.

[317]Ibid., 57 and 64.

[318]*Annual Reports: City of Atlanta, 1895.*

[319]*Annual Reports: City of Atlanta, 1896*, 54.

[320]Ibid; *Annual Reports: City of Atlanta, 1905*, 50.

[321]*Annual Reports: City of Atlanta, 1895*, 39.

[322]*Annual Reports: City of Atlanta, 1905*, 50.

[323]Knight, *Reminiscences of Famous Georgians*, 2:502–3.

[324]Ibid.

[325]Fulton County Court of Ordinary, Record of Wills, GDAH, 1910.

[326]Hugh Inman Richardson, interview by Jo Ann Warmack, 11 July 1976, Inman Genealogy File, AHC.

[327]*Atlanta Constitution*, 17 April 1931.

[328]Ibid.

[329]Atlanta City Council Minutes, 8 March 1917.

[330]*Atlanta Constitution*, 17 April 1931.

[331]Garrett, *Atlanta and Environs*, 2:638.

[332]Hugh T. Inman to John W. Grant, August 12 1910, AHC, Inman, Grant and Slaton Family Papers.

[333]Ibid.

[334]Ibid.

[335]Ibid. Garrett, *Atlanta and Environs*, 2:562 and 2:573.

[336]*Atlanta Journal*, 11 July 1918.

[337]Garrett, *Atlanta and Environs*, 2:755.

[338]Ibid., 2:107.

[339]Northen, *Men of Mark*, 4:232.

[340]Inman Genealogy File, AHC.

[341]Deaton, "Atlanta During the Progressive Era," 460.

[342]Ibid., 458.

[343]*Atlanta Constitution*, 9 March 1938.

[344]Doyle, *New Men*, 152 and 157.

[345]Russell, *Atlanta*, 234.

[346]*Atlanta Constitution*, 13 March 1881. Doyle, *New Men*, 153.

[347]Garrett, *Atlanta and Environs*, 2:30.

[348]Doyle, *New Men*, 155.

[349]Russell, *Atlanta*, 235. *Atlanta Constitution*, 13 March 1881.

[350]*Atlanta Constitution*, 13 December 1881.

[351]Ibid., 6 October 1881.

[352]Ibid., 1 December 1881.

[353]Ibid., 13 December 1881.

[354]Ibid., 9 October 1887.

[355]Garrett, *Atlanta and Environs*, 2:313–15.

[356]Doyle, *New Men*, 267.

[357]Garrett, *Atlanta and Environs*, 2:315.

[358]Ibid.

[359]Samuel Martin Inman Scrapbook, AHC.

[360]Garrett, *Atlanta and Environs*, 2:316.

[361]*Atlanta Constitution*, 23 November 1895.

[362]*Annual Reports: City of Atlanta, 1896*, 39.

[363]Doyle, *New Men*, 267.

[364]Garrett, *Atlanta and Environs*, 2:319.

[365]*Atlanta Constitution*, 23 November 1895.

[366]Ibid., 5 November 1895.

[367]Ibid., 8 November 1895.

[368]Ibid., 23 November 1895.

[369]Ibid., 5 November 1895. Ibid., 15 June 1906.

[370]Doyle, *New Men*, 151.

[371]Ibid., 46.

[372]*Memoirs of Georgia*, 1:833. Martin, *Atlanta and Its Builders*, 2:372. Davis, *Henry Grady*, 209, n. 7.

[373]Martin, *Atlanta and Its Builders*, 2:372.

[374]Northen, *Men of Mark*, 4:231.

[375]Davis, *Henry Grady*, 23.

[376]Ibid., 175.

[377]Raymond B. Nixon, *Henry W. Grady: Spokesman of the New South* (New York: Alfred A. Knopf, 1943) 239–40.

[378]George B. Tindall, *The Emergence of the New South* (Baton Rouge: University of Louisiana, 1967) 2–3.

[379]Ibid., 49.

[380]Edward H. Inman Personality File, AHC. Inman Genealogy File, AHC.

[381]*Atlanta Constitution*, 17 April 1931.

[382]*The Americana: A Universal Reference Library. Biographies* (New York: Americana Corporation, 1933) 80.

[383]*Atlanta Journal*, 9 March 1938.

[384]"Red Cross Briefs," vol. 1, February 1921, Atlanta Chapter of the American Red Cross, AHC.

[385]Garrett, *Atlanta and Environs*, 3:244.

[386]Kate Richardson Lumpkin Papers, Printed Material on the Women's Council of National Defense, Georgia Division, AHC.

[387]Ibid.

[388]Ibid.

[389]Elizabeth Hunt, *American National Red Cross: Metropolitan Atlanta Chapter 1914–1979* (self published, 1979) 8.

[390]Ibid., 9.

[391]Harold H. Martin, *Atlanta and Environs: A Chronicle of Its People & Events. Years of Change & Challenge, 1940–1976* 4 vols. (Atlanta: The Atlanta Historical Society, 1987) 3: 325.

[392]Hunt, *American National Red Cross*, 11–12.

[393]Ibid., 14.

[394]American Red Cross, Atlanta Chapter, Records, AHC.

[395]Ibid.

[396]Ibid.

[397]Doyle, *New Men*, xv.

[398]Ibid., 19.

[399]Samuel Martin Inman Personality File.

[400]*The Americana: A Universal Reference Library. Biographies* (New York: Americana Corporation, 1933).

[401]Edward H. Inman Personality File, AHC.

[402]Bryant, *Capital City Club*, 67.

[403]Annie M. Inman to Josephine Van Dyke Inman, 7 October 1889, AHC, Inman, Grant and Slaton Family Papers.

[404]Inman Genealogy File, AHC.

[405]Margaret V. D. Grant to Margaret J. Van Dyke Inman, 29 January 1911, AHC, Inman, Grant and Slaton Family Papers. Anne I. Grant to Annie M. Inman Grant, 5 October 1919, AHC, Inman, Grant and Slaton Family Papers.

[406]*Atlanta Constitution*, 13 January 1915.

[407]Bryant, *Capital City Club*, 35.

[408]Jack Blicksilver, "The International Cotton Exposition of 1881 & Its Impact upon the Economic Development of Georgia," *Atlanta Economic Review* (June 1957): 12.

[409]Robert C. McMath, *Engineering the New South: Georgia Tech-1885–1985* (Athens: University of Georgia Press, 1985) 26.

[410]Ibid., 29.

[411]*Atlanta Constitution*, 1 October 1885.

[412]Bryant, *Capital City Club*, 35.

[413]McMath, *Engineering the New South*, 46.

[414]*Atlanta Constitution*, 6 October 1888.

[415]*Atlanta Georgian*, 15 January 1915.

[416]*Atlanta Constitution*, 9 March 1938.

[417]McMath, *Engineering the New South*, 111.

[418]Ibid., 90.

[419]Walter Edward McNair, *Lest We Forget: An Account of Agnes Scott College* (Atlanta: Tucker-Castleberry Printing, Inc., 1983) 2.

[420]Ibid., 12.

[421]Agnes Scott College Board of Trustee Minutes, 13 October 1903, 31 December 1914, 9 February 1904, ASC.

[422]Ibid., 31 December 1914.

[423]"Agnes Scott College Bulletin," Memorial Number-Samuel Martin Inman, February 1915, 5.

[424]McNair, *Lest We Forget,* 31.

[425]Agnes Scott College Board of Trustee Minutes, 1889–1914, ASC.

[426]*Atlanta: Yesterday, Today and Tomorrow,* 248.

[427]Samuel Martin Inman Personality File, AHC.

[428]Ibid.

[429]Jane Walker Inman Personality File, AHC.

[430]Samuel Martin Inman Scrapbook, AHC.

[431]*Atlanta Journal,* 26 March 1908.

[432]Garrett, *Atlanta and Environs,* 2:596.

[433]*Atlanta Constitution,* 15 January 1915.

[434]Garrett, *Atlanta and Environs,* 2:596.

[435]J. K. Orr, interview by Evelyn Yates Inman, 1926, Arthur Crew Inman Collection, AHC.

[436]Mary Van Dyke Battey, interview by Evelyn Yates Inman, 1926, Arthur Crew Inman Collection, AHC. *General Catalogue of Atlanta University, 1867–1929* (Atlanta: Atlanta University Press, 1929) 7. Myron W. Adams, *A History of Atlanta University* (Atlanta: Atlanta University Press, 1930).

[437]*Atlanta Constitution,* 15 January 1915.

[438]Ibid., 86.

[439]Doyle, *New Men,* 30.

[440]Howell, *The Book of Georgia,* 553. Samuel M. Inman Personality File, AHC. Exact dates on these events are have to determine since they took place over a span of years.

[441]"Agnes Scott College Bulletin," Memorial Number–Samuel Martin Inman, February 1915, 10.

[442] Samuel Martin Inman Personality File, AHC.

[443]*The City Builder,* December 1923, 32–34.

[444]*Atlanta Journal,* 9 December 1964.

[445]Martin, *Atlanta and Environs,* 3:47.

[446]Colonial Dames of America, Atlanta Chapter, Minutes, AHC.

[447]Coleman, *A History of Georgia,* 279.

[448]Clifford M. Kuhn, Harlon E. Joye, and E. Bernard West, *Living Atlanta: An Oral History of the City, 1914–1948* (Athens: University of Georgia Press, 1990) 37.

[449]John M. Slaton to Sarah F. Grant Slaton, 25 September 1906, AHC, Inman, Grant and Slaton Family Papers.

[450]Ibid.

[451]Ibid.

[452]*Atlanta Constitution*, 4 January 1907.

[453]Ibid.

[454]Ibid.

[455]Ibid.

[456]Ibid.

[457]*Atlanta Georgian*, 18 November 1910.

[458]Ibid.

[459]Ibid.

[460]*Atlanta Constitution*, 16 November 1910.

[461]Ibid.

[462]Ibid.

[463]Doyle, *New Men*, 96.

[464]Ibid., 94.

[465]Ibid., 93.

[466]Ibid., 98 and 249.

[467]Ibid., 98.

[468]George B. Tindall, *The Emergence of the New South, 1913–1945* (Baton Rouge: University of Louisiana, 1967) 20.

[469]Garrett, *Atlanta and Environs*, 2: 96.

[470]Davis, *Henry Grady*, 47–8.

[471]First Presbyterian Church of Atlanta Records, GDAH.

[472]"Agnes Scott College Bulletin" Memorial Number-Samuel Martin Inman, February 1915.

[473]*Atlanta Journal*, 26 November 1921. Oakland Cemetery has several family burial plots of the Inmans, including Shadrach W. Inman's, Hugh T. Inman's, Samuel M. Inman's, Hugh Richardson's, and the Grant family's mausoleum. On Hugh's family plot there are two marble cherub sculptures, each in remembrance of his young children who died, are included on the cemetery's visitor's guide.

[474]First Presbyterian Church of Atlanta Records, 1886, GDAH.

[475]*Atlanta Constitution*, 9 March 1938.

[476]*Reminiscences of Famous Georgians*, 2:503.

[477]John W. Grant, interview by Evelyn Yates Inman, 1926, Arthur Crew Inman Collection, AHC. *Atlanta Constitution*, 28 November 1921.

[478]Fulton County Court of Ordinary, Record of Wills, 1907, GDAH.

[479]H. Frank West, interview by Evelyn Yates Inman, 1926, Arthur Crew Inman Collection, AHC.

[480]Jane Walker Inman Personality File, AHC.

[481]Northen, *Men of Mark*, 4:232. Fulton County Court of Ordinary, Record of Wills, 1907, GDAH.

[482]William Bailey Williford, *Peachtree Street, Atlanta* (Athens: University of Georgia Press) 91.

[483]*Atlanta Journal*, 9 December 1964. *Notable Men of Atlanta*, Atlanta, 1913.

[484]Annie M. Inman to Margaret J. Van Dyke Inman, 15 August 1889, AHC, Inman, Grant and Slaton Family Papers.

[485]*Atlanta Constitution,* 20 September 1892; *Atlanta Journal,* 20 September 1892.

[486]*Atlanta Georgian,* 15 January 1915.

[487]Ibid. See Appendix C for photo.

[488]Ibid.; *Atlanta Constitution,* 20 September 1892.

[489]*Atlanta Constitution,* 20 September 1892. *Atlanta Journal,* 20 September 1892.

[490]Atlanta City Council Minutes, 21 August 1893.

[491]Ibid., 28 October 1895.

[492]Ibid., 4 November 1895, 20 January 1896, 6 February 1896.

[493]Ibid., 17 October 1892.

[494]Ibid., 20 August 1894.

[495]*Atlanta Journal,* 30 May 1896.

[496]H. Frank West, interview by Evelyn Yates Inman, 1926, Arthur Crew Inman Collection, AHC.

[497]Mary Van Dyke Battey, interview by Evelyn Yates Inman, 1926, Arthur Crew Inman Collection, AHC.

[498]Garrett, *Atlanta and Environs,* 2:193–94. *Atlanta Journal,* 22 January 1901.

[499]Ibid., 2:256.

[500]Ibid., 2:258.

[501]Atlanta City Council Minutes, 7 March 1892.

[502]Ibid., 30 December 1897.

[503]Fulton County Court of Ordinary, Record of Wills, 1910, GDAH.

[504]Ibid., 1907.

[505]*The City Builder,* December 1923, 32–34. Samuel M. Inman Scrapbook, AHC.

[506]Emily Caroline MacDougald Inman Personality File, AHC.

[507]Doyle, *New Men, 221.*

[508]Garrett, *Atlanta and Environs,* 2:480.

[509]Atlanta Art Association, Printed Press Release and Association Records, AHC.

[510]Ibid.

[511]Ibid.

[512]Ibid.

[513]Ibid.

[514]Ibid.

[515]Ibid.

[516]*Atlanta Constitution,* 9 March 1938.

[517]Ibid.

[518]Ibid.

[519]Atlanta Music Festival Association Subject File, AHC.

[520]Doyle, *New Men,* 222.

[521]Atlanta Music Festival Association Subject File, AHC.

[522]*Atlanta Journal,* 9 March 1938.

[523]Garrett, *Atlanta and Environs,* 2:760.

[524]Doyle, *New Men*, 189.

[525]Ibid., 223.

[526]Anne Firor Scott, *Natural Allies: Women's Associations in American History* (Urbana: University of Illinois Press, 1992) 80 and 141.

[527]Ibid., 81.

[528]Ibid., 135.

[529]Doyle, *New Men*, 223.

[530]Scott, *Natural Allies*, 129–133.

[531]Annie M. Inman Grant to Margaret J. Van Dyke Inman, 1893, AHC, Inman, Grant and Slaton Family Papers.

[532]Darlene Rebecca Roth, *Matronage: Patterns in Women's Organizations, Atlanta, Georgia, 1890–1940* (New York: Carlson Publishing, Inc., 1994) 36.

[533]Doyle, *New Men*, 223.

[534]Anne Firor Scott, *The Southern Lady: From Pedestal to Politics, 1830–1930* (Chicago: University of Chicago Press, 1970) 111.

[535]Scott, *Natural Allies*, 140.

[536]Ibid. Doyle, *New Men*, 214.

[537]Martin, *Atlanta and Environs*, 3:54.

[538]Musical Association Papers, GDAH.

[539]Emily Caroline MacDougald Inman Personality File, AHC.

[540]Young Women's Christian Association to Sarah F. Grant Slaton, 11 March 1909, AHC, Inman, Grant and Slaton Family Papers. Chamber of Commerce Expansion Campaign to Sarah F. Grant Slaton, 23 February 1920, AHC, Inman, Grant and Slaton Family Papers.

[541]Garrett, *Atlanta and Environs*, 2:762.

[542]Ibid., 2:137.

[543]*Atlanta Constitution*, 14 September 1887.

[544]Garrett, *Atlanta and Environs*, 2:156.

[545]Ibid., 2:455.

[546]Bryant, *Capital City Club*, 67 and 42.

[547]Garrett, *Atlanta and Environs*, 2:576.

[548]*Atlanta Constitution*, 17 April 1931. Inman Genealogy File, AHC. *The Americana*, 80.

[549]Ibid.

[550]Ibid. *Atlanta Journal*, 17 April 1931. Inman Genealogy File, AHC.

[551]*Atlanta Journal*, 24 July 1909.

[552]Atlanta City Council Minutes, 19 February 1906.

[553]Garrett, *Atlanta and Environs*, 2:241.

[554]Ibid., 2:546–47.

[555]Doyle, *New Men*, 98.

[556]*News* (Savannah GA), 16 November 1910.

[557]Garrett, *Atlanta and Environs*, 2:179.

[558]Samuel Martin Inman Personality File, AHC.

[559]Doyle, *New Men*, 20.

[560]Ibid., xiv.

INDEX